AN
UNLIKELY
REVOLUTIONARY

EXTRAORDINARY LIVES
The Experience of Hawai'i Nisei

General editor, Dennis M. Ogawa

The purpose of this series is to preserve in authoritative editions the life stories of the nisei in Hawai'i. The series represents the nisei experience in a broad range of areas, including culture and the arts, family and community, and business and politics. By doing so, it attempts to address universal questions of identity, gender, values, justice, and culture. Each work is based on primary source material (autobiographies, diaries, letters, oral histories) authorized by the individuals themselves or their heirs. Each work also includes an introduction that provides important social and historical contexts and explains the significance of the individual's life for a fuller understanding of modern Hawai'i.

AN UNLIKELY REVOLUTIONARY

Matsuo Takabuki and the
Making of Modern Hawai'i

a memoir by
Matsuo Takabuki
assisted by Dennis M. Ogawa
with Glen Grant and Wilma Sur

University of Hawai'i Press
Honolulu

*For Aya, Glen, Beth, Anne,
and the grandchildren*

© 1998 University of Hawai'i Press
All rights reserved
Printed in the United States of America
03 02 01 00 99 98   5 4 3 2 1

Takabuki, Matsuo, 1923–
    An unlikely revolutionary : Matsuo Takabuki and the making of
modern Hawai'i : a memoir / by Matsuo Takabuki.
        p.   cm.
    Includes index.
    ISBN 0–8248–2023–1 (alk. paper). — ISBN 0–8248–2083–5 (pbk. :
alk. paper)
        1. Takabuki, Matsuo, 1923–   . 2. Politicians—Hawaii—Biography.
    3. Hawaii—Politics and government—1950–   I. Title.
    DU627.83.T35A3   1998
    996.9'03'092—dc21
    [B]   97–48949
                                                                                    CIP

University of Hawai'i Press books are printed on acid-free
paper and meet the guidelines for permanence and durability
of the Council on Library Resources

Designed by David C. denBoer, Nighthawk Design

Publication of this book has been supported by a subsidy from the
University of Hawai'i Foundation Hawai'i Nisei Publication Fund.

Contents

Acknowledgments

I SOMETIMES WONDER why this book needed to be written. I did not care to respond to the many things written about me, largely uncomplimentary, in books and newspapers. I treasure my privacy too much, and I do not have an egotistical urge to do a book on myself. I still wonder who would care about my life and my views on Hawai'i, the mainland, and the Pacific Rim.

I began this project at the urging of many friends, particularly University of Hawai'i professor Dennis M. Ogawa, and Makoto Iida and Juichi Toda, both of Secom Company, Ltd., Japan. These individuals persuaded me that I had an obligation to chronicle, from my perspective, some of the events that I have witnessed and been part of in the development of modern Hawai'i. Although I still do not believe that my views merit special attention, it is true that fate has placed me in a position to view and evaluate events of historical interest in Hawai'i. Consequently, my personal experiences may assist readers to understand some of the issues and how and why we acted as we did in shaping and transforming Hawai'i over the past fifty years. In this respect, I hope the book will be informative and worthwhile.

Many people generously assisted in this project. I am obligated especially to the trustees, staff, and business associates I worked with at Kamehameha Schools/Bishop Estate, and to my friends in the Pacific Rim and on the mainland United States. In addition to Professor Ogawa, I am also indebted to Glen Grant and Wilma Sur for doing extensive interviews of people and assisting on the manuscript, and Sharon Yamamoto of the University of Hawai'i Press for her editorial supervision.

AN
UNLIKELY
REVOLUTIONARY

Introduction

By Dennis M. Ogawa and Glen Grant

"Social revolutionary" is not a term that one would normally associate with Matsuo ("Matsy") Takabuki. Well-known in the Hawaiian Islands over the past four decades as a financial and political leader, Takabuki has been largely viewed as a prominent member of the island establishment. Actively involved in the Democratic Party in the post–World War II years, he was among a generation of Americans of Japanese ancestry in the islands to rise to political power in the 1950s, serving for sixteen years on the Board of Supervisors of the City and County of Honolulu. For many years a confidant to Governor John Burns, Takabuki was given the nickname "Taisho" or "Boss" within the governor's inner circle. Working with island entrepreneur Chinn Ho, Takabuki was also involved in some of the most important financial projects during the island development boom of the 1960s and 1970s, including the construction of the Ilikai Hotel, the first major condominium built in Hawai'i. For over twenty-one years he served as a trustee of the Bishop Estate, Hawai'i's largest private landowner that oversees Kamehameha Schools, one of the wealthiest private schools in the nation. From Wall Street to the financial centers of Tokyo and Hong Kong, Matsy Takabuki has been involved in multimillion-dollar negotiations that have helped connect Hawai'i to several international business investments. If the term "social revolutionary" implies

1

an anti-establishment radical who wishes to uproot and overturn the status quo, then Takabuki must definitely represent the opposite end of the political spectrum—a political and financial figure of extraordinary influence who has been at the center of island governance for nearly a half century.

The description of Matsy Takabuki as a social revolutionary seems, then, wholly inappropriate for someone who has been described by some critics as a "power broker" or "kingpin"[1] of the island community. Yet in the historical context of his life, which spans nearly three-quarters of the twentieth century, Takabuki has been a leading player in a series of sweeping social, financial, and political changes that have fundamentally altered Hawai'i's racial and class structures. Whatever critical perspective the historian brings to the experiences of nisei, or second-generation Japanese Americans, in the era following World War II, one overriding reality remains unaltered: the severe racial limitations placed on this generation before and during the war were deliberately attacked and successfully lifted so as to allow a new rising ethnic group to achieve an economically and socially more secure place in island society. While the ultimate goal of this generation was not to destroy the basic structures of Hawai'i or to throw out capitalism, their efforts to gain greater access to existing systems enervated the old sugar oligarchy and heralded a period of racial and class diversification. The process was far from equal for members of this generation. A few Japanese Americans such as Takabuki attained great degrees of power and influence during this period while others struggled in working-class conditions hindered by low wages, a high cost of living, and stagnant opportunity. However, when measured by the rising number of Japanese Americans entering the professional occupations after the 1950s, the expansion of small business operations in tourism and the service industry during the boom years of the 1960s and 1970s, and the rising personal and family incomes of the ethnic group in the islands,

1. Noel Kent, *Hawai'i: Islands under the Influence* (Honolulu: University of Hawai'i Press, 1993), p. 151.

Takabuki and his contemporaries had indeed been unlikely revolutionaries in spearheading a tremendous change in Hawaiian life. They were catalysts for the emergence of a bona fide middle class for the first time in Hawai'i since the introduction of a foreign economic system a century earlier.

The concept of middle class in the context of 1950 Hawai'i, however, goes beyond the attainment of a certain income level or financial security. Nor can it be measured solely in terms of being able to pay the mortgage on one's home. Middle-class status for this generation meant having economic choice—being independent enough from a paternalistic plantation system to be able to attain employment in whatever profession one might choose and to rise to a level commensurate with one's ability, not racial complexion. To identify oneself with a middle-class lifestyle was dependent on one's ability to have choices in employment, career advancement, and home ownership.

The Hawai'i into which Matsy Takabuki was born in 1923 had no significant middle class. Since the introduction of large-scale Western capital into the Hawaiian Islands with the advent of the sugar industry in the 1860s, the island social system had been characterized by a clear demarcation between master and servants, rich and poor. The sugar plantations and related companies eventually comprising the Big Five were largely owned by an Anglo-Saxon minority comprising less than 10 percent of the islands' population. The Native Hawaiian population, eventually dispossessed of land, governance, and language, were relegated to working-class occupations in the towns or poor tenant farming. The thousands of immigrant laborers from Asia, the Pacific, and Europe who were imported into the islands worked for meager wages under a strictly controlled, racially biased system. By the end of the nineteenth century, when the islands were annexed to the United States, this racial and economic caste system was fully entrenched, allowing a *haole* or Caucasian minority to "divide and rule" the islands with a strong fist of legal and economic enforcement when required and a beneficent sense of paternalism when convenient.

Many foreign laborers working on Hawai'i's plantations eagerly sought to better their lives by leaving the sugar fields for opportunities in Honolulu or other urban centers. Carpentry, plumbing, blacksmithing, and other trades were available to the more independent immigrants; a few entered a variety of professional positions open within the various ethnic communities. Some Chinese and Japanese immigrants operated family rice, taro, and coffee farms; others such as the Okinawan immigrants developed piggeries. Matsy Takabuki's father had a trucking business in Waialua. However, the bulk of the non-white population in Hawai'i, comprising over 80 percent of the populace, remained bound to the sugar and pineapple industries, the primary economic employers before World War II. The very best in life that a young man such as Matsy Takabuki could ever hope for in this territorial Hawai'i was possibly a career as a teacher. Without any real opportunities beyond agriculture, a trade, or working for the family business, the prospects of becoming middle class for the majority of these young islanders seemed beyond reach unless they were fortunate enough to enter Teachers College.

The bombs that fell on Pearl Harbor on December 7, 1941, also fell inadvertently on this caste system that had frustrated the ambitions of a generation. The factors that would allow the nisei the opportunity to participate in the creation of a Hawai'i middle class were manifold. Three years of martial law weakened the political control of the Big Five companies, which found themselves sometimes at odds with the military government that had seized power after the attack on Pearl Harbor. A million soldiers passing through the islands introduced islanders of all races to a new kind of *haole*—neither rich nor elitist, these white soldiers formed friendships and sometimes married with the local non-white population. Due to the great number of military and civilian construction personnel in the islands during the war, small businesses owned by Japanese Americans and other locals flourished, servicing the newcomers.

The question of national loyalty that often clouded the nisei's identity before the war as tensions between the United

States and Japan mounted created an emotional imperative during the war. With thousands of other young Japanese American men and women, Matsy Takabuki joined the United States Army, serving in the 442nd Regimental Combat Team and fighting in Europe. This experience opened many of these young men's and women's eyes to the inequities facing non-white Americans throughout the United States. Moreover, surviving the ordeal of combat aroused a sense of commitment to fight racial unfairness in their home islands. Serving in the war further allowed Takabuki and other veterans to pursue higher education at universities and colleges throughout the United States under the GI Bill of Rights. Takabuki himself obtained his law degree from the University of Chicago in 1949.

Armed with an outstanding education and a sense of pride and mission, the returning Japanese American veterans threw themselves into the maelstrom of postwar forces that continued to break down the racial barriers inhibiting the emergence of an island middle class. The fact that the young Takabuki and his wife returned to the islands in 1949 in the midst of the great International Longshoremen and Warehousemens Union (ILWU) dock strike, which for the first time helped significantly improve the lives of sugar industry employees, dramatizes the many opportunities opening up for those willing to take risks.

While Takabuki would perhaps feel comfortable with the description of himself as a calculated risk-taker during this period of his life, he actually denies the label of "revolutionary." In his abrupt, down-to-earth manner, he minimizes the role that Japanese Americans played in the political and economic life of the Hawaiian Islands, preferring to see the process of postwar change as a result of evolution, not revolution. The tremendous social movement in which he participated to transform Hawai'i from a territory under the control of a racial elite to a highly diverse, competitive modern community was a consequence, he stresses, of a gradual process of generational ambition stemming from basic cultural values instilled by both home and school long before the attack on Pearl Harbor. The Japanese American "postwar rise" in the islands was not in his view an effort to uproot the foundations of capitalism or to alter the fundamental system by which power is achieved or distributed. To understand this evolution, Takabuki explains, one must look not only at political strategies or economic investments, but at the values of hard work, loyalty, and perseverance inculcated in the men and women of his generation through their Japanese upbringing and their American education. Tempered by the fire of war, they eagerly sought to earn their place in the island sun without being limited by race or class status. In that evolutionary movement, Takabuki would be the first to state that the old Hawai'i once defined as the "sugar-coated fortress" would be engulfed by the rising tide of middle-class expectations of a diverse, ambitious, and irreverent postwar breed of political entrepreneurs.

Historical scholarship in recent years has increasingly focused on the roles of nisei political and financial leaders such as Matsy Takabuki in the tremendous social upheavals that followed World War II. Lawrence Fuchs in his 1961 study of island social forces, *Hawai'i Pono: A Social History,* interpreted the Japanese American economic and political rise of the 1950s and 1960s as evidence of the forces of equality and racial justice operating within the multicultural community. For Fuchs, the emerging pattern of racial equity was evidence of the prevailing "promise of Hawai'i," that "aloha set a standard of conduct in Hawai'i which many people found difficult to live up to, but which nearly everyone openly approved."[2]

While the Democratic Party election victories of 1954 have been commonly called a "Bloodless Revolution," other recent historians have minimized the socioeconomic consequences of that "revolution," emphasizing instead the business-as-usual way the new politicos sought favor for themselves and friends. Recently published works by Noel Kent (*Hawai'i: Islands under the Influence*) and George Cooper and Gavan Daws (*Land and Power in Hawai'i*) have interpreted this postwar Japanese American rise in far more cynical terms. For

2. Lawrence Fuchs, *Hawai'i Pono: A Social History* (New York: Harcourt, Brace & World, 1961), p. 448.

Kent, the old oligarchy of the Big Five *haole*-based companies that dominated the economy of the Territory of Hawai'i during the first half of the century was merely broadened to include a politically cohesive group of up-and-coming Asian American entrepreneurs who were motivated more by greed than sentiments of social justice. Kent contends that the notion that nisei leaders in the postwar years were motivated by social justice is a "too superficial analysis." Second-generation Japanese Americans, he argues, were inculcated through their public school experience with an "individualistically oriented competitive world view exalting middle class materialistic goals and equating success with wealth, status and power—an education for selfishness and self-aggrandizement in the traditional American sense." The efforts of the nisei in the postwar years to "make it" in island society, Kent therefore argues, was motivated primarily by self-interest and only secondarily with concerns of the world around them as they "enriched themselves."[3]

Cooper and Daws go on to suggest that Democratic Party politicians, including Takabuki, used their newfound legislative power to facilitate extensive land acquisitions and development for the benefit of friends, associates, and themselves. The young rising stars of the Japanese American political scene of the 1950s, in this argument, became involved in a complex series of *hui* or real estate partnerships that often wedded governmental decision-making and land development with racial preferences. For over three decades, Cooper and Daws write, "politically well-connected Democrats have involved themselves, from start to finish, with the full range of buyers, sellers and developers of real estate." Recognizing that there has never been a ruling class in Hawai'i "that has not drawn its strength and sought its continuing advantage from land,"[4] the postwar Democratic Party leaders have become the new ruling elite. For Cooper and Daws, Matsy Takabuki is

3. Kent, *Hawai'i*, p. 130.
4. George Cooper and Gavan Daws, *Land and Power in Hawai'i: The Democratic Years* (Honolulu: Benchmark Books, 1985), p. 14.

clearly one of the approximately 270 men and women who were within this new island oligarchy.

In both the Kent and the Cooper and Daws critiques of the postwar Japanese American rise there seems to be a lingering misconception that this generation was somehow diverted from the basic altruistic goal of achieving social and racial equality to the pursuit of their self-interest at the expense of others. Kent equates this selfishness with their Americanization, neglecting to examine the values of success and material gain that motivated their parents to sojourn to Hawai'i in the first place. Cooper and Daws seem almost surprised that this young, ambitious new Democratic Party force would unite government and business for personal and generational gain as if governments in the United States at local, state, or national levels ever operated wholly insulated from the economic centers of power.

What other strategy of wresting political and economic control would they suggest was open to this generation unabashedly "on the make"? How else could a generation with limited economic means have challenged the Big Five control of the islands unless through a concerted, grassroots-based effort to wield political power and then implement economic measures, including taxation, zoning, and land reform, designed to undermine the old system? The social changes the nisei initiated in the 1950s by the coalition of labor, war veterans, and disempowered islanders under the leadership of John Burns are therefore being attacked for "not going far enough," for "selling out" to developers and capitalists, for not advocating the cause of the working classes from which many of its leaders had emerged.

No matter how critical the view of the postwar rise of the nisei, there is little question that the Hawaiian Islands after 1950 had been radically transformed from the days when "King Sugar" ruled. Even though a new non-white power base had emerged—joining, not wholly replacing, the older Merchant Street oligarchy—the democratization of decision-making had made radical strides from the days when a small minority ruled the islands through interlocking directorates and family influence. Ethnic prejudice and institutional racism unfortunately remained part of the fabric of island life, but the rigid racial barriers once rigorously maintained by the *kamaaina haole* elite without much redress had fallen to a more open and fluid racial climate and economic competition. Most important, the weakening of the sugar industry allowed tourism in spite of all of its drawbacks to open up economic opportunities to small entrepreneurs, permitting a middle class to establish itself in the postwar years.

Attributing all these changes to one ethnic generation or person would, of course, be wildly inaccurate. However, not to acknowledge the significant racial advancements made in the postwar decades because this social movement did not uproot capitalism in the islands or followed traditional patterns of land and power is equally to distort the deep-seated motives of the postwar Hawai'i generation. Cognizant of the racial limitations placed on their lives by the older plantation society, bristling at the ethnic suspicions and accusations leveled at them during World War II, rooted in the economic values of getting ahead and securing a place for themselves and their children, these second-generation Japanese Americans sought social justice and economic opportunity in postwar Hawai'i so that they could fulfill an American Dream that had been denied their parents. To have expected them to radically alter the economic system of the islands would have been a myopic understanding of their entrepreneurial values; to have hoped that they would have declined the temptations of power would have been to deny the scope of their rising expectations.

When the nisei generation has attempted to write about their lives, the result has frequently been criticized as either self-serving or promoting an unrealistic Japanese American Horatio Alger myth. The story of the nisei tends to be told as a struggle from poverty and racism to a position of success thanks to hard work, good family values, and *shikata ga nai*, the sense of endurance or "it cannot be helped." Although a few political leaders such as Senator Daniel Inouye have written their autobiographies, many nisei men and women who played key roles in the postwar years have unfortunately remained largely silent. Of course, the wartime experiences of the nisei generation have been widely acclaimed in such works as John Tsukano's *Bridge of Love,* Dorothy Matsuo's *From Boyhood to War,* and Thelma Chang's *I Can Never Forget.* Tom Ige's *Boy from Kahaluu: An Autobiography* chronicles his life growing up in rural Hawai'i, serving in the Military Intelligence Service (MIS) during World War II, and participating in the political and economic changes of the past four decades. Yet few movers and shakers at the heart of these wide-ranging changes have chronicled from their perspective the events that critically influenced the development of modern Hawai'i.

The fact that Matsy Takabuki was finally persuaded to participate in this current project is fortunate for anyone interested in understanding the past fifty years of Hawaiian history. As George Cooper and Gavan Daws wrote in *Land and Power in Hawai'i,* "It would be historically valuable, and humanly good, to hear about the experiences of those in the first generation of Democratic politics in Hawai'i spelled out firsthand and from the inside, by those who have now made all their public choices and can reflect on their lives."[5] Matsy Takabuki's candid commentary on his experiences as one of the major players of this first generation at the center of island power without question is of immense value to academics, historians, and the general public.

Unlike some biographical subjects who seek out a chronicler, Takabuki had to be literally cajoled into sitting down for a series of lengthy interviews to record his life, work, and views on Hawai'i, Asia, and the Pacific century. Dennis M. Ogawa, professor of American studies at the University of Hawai'i and a long time friend, frequently asked Takabuki to participate in an autobiographical project. Each time he responded characteristically with a terse, self-deprecating refusal. "Who would care about that?" he'd answer.

After his retirement from the Bishop Estate in 1993, Matsy Takabuki was again pressured to begin his autobiography

---

5. Ibid., p. 455.

through the efforts of Makoto Iida, chairman, and Juichi Toda, vice chairman, of Secom Company, Ltd., one of the most respected publicly listed corporations in Japan. Recognizing that Hawai'i plays a critical role in Asian Pacific relations, and that Matsy Takabuki represents an exemplary figure embracing Eastern and Western values, Mr. Toda was especially persistent and finally convinced Takabuki to begin to work with Dr. Ogawa in the effort to record his life story. Takabuki sat down for several hours once a week for three months, answering questions posed by Ogawa, who was assisted by Glen Grant, Wilma Sur, and Arnold Hiura. The questions were developed by first interviewing many of Takabuki's associates at Kamehameha Schools and Bishop Estate, individuals at other nonprofit educational institutions, and various leaders of business establishments in America and Asia. Tape-recordings of Takabuki's interviews were then transcribed, edited, and reorganized for Takabuki's careful scrutiny. With the meticulous concern for detail acquired through his legal training, he then carefully rewrote every transcribed interview and reviewed the various drafts of the completed manuscript at least four times. He also selected several speeches or articles that he had written over the years, which appear here as appendixes. These additional materials, written between 1952 and 1991, provide the reader with primary information on various periods of Takabuki's life and reflect his thoughts on important issues facing the 442nd Regimental Combat Team, the Bishop Estate, and Kamehameha Schools.

During the interview process, Takabuki made one thing quite clear: he did not want this work to be simply an autobiography. Downplaying his own role in the history of Japanese Americans in Hawai'i, he stressed that his life was no different than that of any other young Japanese American growing up in rural Hawai'i before the war. While he loved and honored his immigrant parents, the values of loyalty, obligation, and patriotism inculcated in those years, he believed, were not unique to his experience. He was simply one of thousands who were heirs to these collective attitudes and behaviors shaped through the interaction of two rich heritages.

Neither did he believe that his World War II record was particularly dramatic. Except perhaps for a short stint playing a Japanese soldier being killed in a U.S. Army war training film, his war stories, he emphasized, were not out-of-the-ordinary. "I'm no war hero," he often told the interviewers who had hoped for a few heart-wrenching tales of bravery on the battlefields of Europe. As a member of the 442nd Regimental Combat Team, which earned the accolade of the most decorated military unit in American history, wartime heroism was perhaps expected of all the veterans. "Being there" was sufficient to ingrain in him—with other nisei veterans and non-veterans—a burning desire to transform their island home in the postwar years. Fighting for freedom abroad, he realized, should earn him the right to struggle for freedom at home. Yet had not this story already been told by others? He insisted that his narrative not be devoted to war stories.

During the postwar years, from the time that he took advantage of the GI Bill of Rights and enrolled in an accelerated law degree program at the University of Chicago, the career of Matsy Takabuki was often meritorious. After his return to the islands in 1949, he worked for the territorial Department of Labor before finally opening up a law practice in downtown Honolulu. Having been student body president at Waialua High School, he was willing to assume leadership positions. After serving as president of the 442nd Veterans Club, he emerged in 1952 as one of the first nisei postwar Democratic politicians to win a seat on the Board of Supervisors of the City and County of Honolulu. Within the power structure of the city administration, he worked in concert with the territorial legislature to create the successful Democratic Party leadership, which over forty years later still dominates island politics. Matsy Takabuki was at the political pulse of the Hawaiian Islands for two decades as the close personal friend and Party associate of Governor John Burns, helping create the so-called rise of the nisei at midcentury and initiate statehood for Hawai'i.

The interviews quickly revealed, however, that these life experiences, the political aspect of Takabuki's career, held no interest to him twenty years later. An intensely private man with a reluctance to be in the media limelight, he had been relieved to leave elective office and enter the world of finance; extracting his memories of key political battles was nearly impossible. He was reluctant to pass judgment on his past political enemies, dismissing the opportunity to use this work as his own sounding board to defend himself against his critics and foes. Despite what could be interpreted on first impression as Takabuki being a blunt if not slightly arrogant person, behind the facade is an individual who is wholly confident in his accomplishments without the need to boast or defend his past actions. Takabuki, the interviewers learned, is also a staunchly loyal friend who recognizes that in the volatile world of politics, charm and finesse mean little unless backed up by courage—in fact, his favorite book is *Profiles in Courage* by John F. Kennedy. His admiration for those politicians who risked their careers to make necessary but unpopular decisions thus seems unsurprising.

Nor would this narrative, Takabuki insisted, deal with any of his personal family affairs. While his wife and children are occasionally mentioned in his narration, when pressed to share more intimate details concerning his family, he always brushed the questions off with a blunt, "That is nobody's business."

Indulging memories of his early years, retelling war stories, refighting old political battles, and sharing private family sentiments were clearly not the primary subjects that aroused Takabuki's interest in this project. What he wanted to discuss—and the discussions were lively, far-reaching, and often meteoric excursions into the world of number-crunchers—were his years of financial experience from Merchant Street to Wall Street, his involvement with overseas investments in Japan, China, and Hong Kong, his commitment to the financial success of the Bishop Estate, his understanding of the educational philosophy of Kamehameha Schools, his observations on U.S.-Asian relations, and his views on the challenges facing Hawai'i in the twenty-first century. While the interviewers may have been motivated by a desire to chronicle the past, Takabuki was far more interested in presenting his observations on the financial forces that continually recreate present-day Hawai'i.

At heart an entrepreneur, Takabuki in this work presents a fresh perspective on the nisei story as told by others who focus on the perspective of family life, cultural values, World War II, or political alliances. As an internationally respected financier, Takabuki is able to provide a firsthand understanding of the economic forces that helped create a middle class in the islands' postwar years. While the emergence of the Democratic Party in the 1950s and 1960s has received some historical attention, this transformation of the island economy during the same period has received far less scrutiny. Viewing Hawai'i from the eyes of Matsy Takabuki working with Chinn Ho and Sam Silverman, the builders of the Ilikai and pioneers of island condominium development, a unique historical portrait emerges of economic activists tearing down the walls of the old oligarchy, which in the process created greater opportunity for others as well as monetary rewards. Takabuki's role in helping restructure financing in the islands, promoting small contractors, and stimulating business entrepreneurs represents as important a change in Hawai'i's rise of the middle class as the elections of 1954.

Perhaps there was no greater opportunity for Matsy Takabuki to serve as a mover and shaker of financial power in Hawai'i than during his tenure as a trustee of the Bishop Estate. The announcement of his appointment to the Estate generated a firestorm of protest that led to street demonstrations, angry Native Hawaiian assemblies, a torrent of letters to the editors, and even death threats. Throughout the controversy he kept quiet, recognizing that his appointment to the largest private estate in the islands dedicated to the support of Kamehameha Schools for Hawaiian children would be guaranteed to arouse racial suspicions and jealousies. With faith in the goodwill of the community and loyalty to those who had appointed him, Takabuki remained steadfast in his refusal to withdraw and served over twenty-one years as one of the most influential trustees on the board.

The 1970s and 1980s were challenging decades to a land-rich, cash-poor estate that supported a major educational institution with proceeds from its leases. Islanders who sought private home ownership saw the large, land-based estates as oppressive landlords. Hawaiians eager for social change looked to the Bishop Estate and Kamehameha Schools for expanded educational programs and opportunities for advancement. Pressured to liquidate their lands to survive, with the financial guidance of Trustee Takabuki, Bishop Estate began reprioritizing its portfolio, reassessing its landholdings, and acquiring new investments that would build a strong, diversified financial base. Twenty years later, the once cumbersome economic dinosaur has become a vibrant, multibillion-dollar organization with investments ranging from China to Wall Street. While Matsy Takabuki's role in the transition of the Bishop Estate still remains controversial even after his retirement, his impact on the long-term economic stability of the Hawaiian institution cannot be questioned. Jon Corzine, managing partner of Goldman Sachs at the time Bishop Estate's investment in that institution was negotiated, said of Takabuki:

> He wasn't seeking an outcome that would end up laying a framework that was going to fail. I think he was more interested in how this was going to work over time in the interest of the Estate. He was not interested in ending up with a lot of conflicts because somebody had been tricky in the negotiations. He was willing to accept that we were both operating under the same basis and that was a good way to deal.[6]

Looking to the twenty-first-century development of the Asian Pacific Rim nations, Takabuki has also contributed to East–West relations as a frequent international financial advisor. Committed to the belief that any international business deal will fail without the mutual recognition of cultural values, traditions, and practices, he has worked on both sides of

6. Interview with Jon Corzine, October 1994, New York City.

the Pacific to enhance cultural understanding and cooperation. Recognizing the danger of what he calls the "WASPY"
attitude of some Americans, he has consistently served as a
bridge between the beliefs and attitudes of Asia and the needs
and interests of the United States and Hawai'i. Few Americans have earned the respect that Matsy Takabuki enjoys as a
non-white American in Beijing, Hong Kong, and Tokyo. Mr.
Sueaki Takaoka, vice chairman of Seibu, one of Japan's leading corporate groups, said to the interviewers:

> We were very fortunate to work with Mr. Takabuki. Of
> course, he is American and I understand that he has a great
> love of Americans, but at the same time he has Japanese roots
> and he has such love for the Japanese people. Mr. Takabuki
> provided us with knowledge on how to do business in Amer-
> ica, but he had those core feelings toward the Japanese people
> which made it very enjoyable to do business with him.[7]

The fact that Takabuki has finally written his memoirs of a
lifetime spent at the heart of Hawai'i will be welcome news to
the historian who seeks a personal perspective on the pivotal
points in Hawai'i's recent history. Of course, an autobiographical work of this nature is history through the biased view of
a participant. As another prominent lawyer, the famed crimi-
nal defense lawyer Clarence Darrow, once wrote as a preface
to his own autobiography, "Autobiography is never entirely
true. No one can get the right perspective on himself. Every
fact is colored by imagination and dream."[8] The value of autobiography, then, is not that it provides historical fact, but
that it sensitizes the reader to the emotional and personal
context of history.

Although Takabuki's words are not necessarily eloquent,
they are as honest, straightforward, and well informed as the
man himself. Even if his observations do not always reveal

---

7. Interview with Sueaki Takaoka, January 27, 1994, Honolulu, Hawai'i.
8. Clarence Darrow, *The Story of My Life* (New York: De Capo Press, 1996),
p. 6.

much of his private side, his candid comments on Hawai'i, the Bishop Estate, Asia Pacific relations, and the future are certain to stir much discussion in the island community, where his name is still synonymous with high finance, land, and power.

After his retirement from the Bishop Estate, Takabuki received a card from a Hawaiian friend who simply wrote that few individuals are ever blessed with the opportunity to make a difference in the lives of others. "You made a difference," she told him. How future generations will assess that difference and its lasting impact on Hawai'i is entirely a matter of speculation. Takabuki does not articulate any justification for what he has done, but believes that the rightness of his actions speaks louder than words. One of his favorite quotes is from a beleaguered Abraham Lincoln, who was often criticized for his style of leadership during the tragic Civil War. "I do the best I know," Lincoln once said during a period of intense national criticism, "the very best I can, and I mean to keep right on doing so until the end. If the end brings me out all right, what is said against me will not amount to anything. If the end brings me out wrong, ten angels swearing I was right would make no difference."[9]

Matsy Takabuki has spent a lifetime in the busy arenas of politics and finance that have helped create modern Hawai'i. This "unlikely revolutionary" stands confident that the legacy of his generation to improve the lives of future islanders will remain secure, with or without Lincoln's swearing angels.

9. Francis Carpenter, *Six Months at the White House* (1867), pp. 258–59, as quoted in *Respectfully Quoted: A Dictionary of Quotations from the Library of Congress* (Washington, D.C.: Congressional Press, 1992), p. 24.

Keiki o Ka Aina

THE MAGNIFICENT Great Hall of China in Beijing was filled
with government officials of the People's Bank of China, the
Central Bank of China, and the Central Bank of the People's
Republic of China, Asian business leaders, and representatives
of the Pacific Rim institutions that had joined together to create the first international joint venture bank in this communist nation. The Great Hall was the historic setting where the
various partners in the venture formally documented, signed,
and commemorated the beginning of this new era in China's
financial international relations. In this place two decades earlier, President Richard M. Nixon in 1972 had officially reestab-
lished relations between the United States and the People's Republic of China. Now, a second-generation Japanese American,
born of poor immigrant parents on a Hawaiian sugar plantation, was about to join the long list of dignitaries who had
stood at the Great Hall's podium to signify an important historical event in U.S.-Sino relations.

As a trustee of the Bishop Estate, one of Hawai'i's major
nonprofit trusts dedicated to providing for the education of Hawaiian children, I was honored to represent the Estate at the
Great Hall ceremonies. The Estate had been invited to participate with the Asian Development Bank and the Long Term
Credit Bank of Japan as the U.S. component in the creation of
the Xiamen International Bank in the People's Republic of
China. An operating bank with headquarters in Xiamen, the
Xiamen International Bank had in addition two subsidiaries: a
retail bank in Macao and a small finance company in Hong

Kong. The bank had become profitable under the leadership of Eugene Ho, a young, bilingual banking professional who had graduated from the University of Chicago. To expand its operation, however, the bank needed additional capital. Consequently, the Xiamen International Bank was to be the first joint venture bank with foreign investors approved by the People's Bank of China and the Central National Government.

From the point of view of the Bishop Estate, the opportunity seemed like a safe and conservative investment with highly credible institutions such as the Asian Development Bank and Long Term Credit Bank of Japan as partners. Each of the foreign investors had a seat on the board of directors with the PRC partners of the bank so that they would be able to participate in and monitor the operation of the bank.

Being the first foreign joint venture bank approved by the Central Bank and the National Government, the closing for our investments was officially set to be in the Great Hall of China, hosted by the People's Bank of China. The ceremony was to be a "showpiece" by the Central Government of a joint venture with credible foreign investors. Since foreign investment in China had been suspended a few years earlier after the Tiananmen Square episode, this official approval of international financing was a small but significant step in the easing of tensions between China and the rest of the world.

Before we officially signed the agreement in the Great Hall, a few representatives of the foreign investors were taken to a smaller room to have a special audience with Li Peng, premier of the National Government. Afterward, we entered the historic hall, where the signing ceremony took place with great pomp and circumstance. A dinner was served in the Great Hall during which several speeches were delivered. Along with the Chinese chairman of the board of directors of the bank, a representative from each of the foreign investment groups was asked to address the gathering. I spoke for our group in English, my message being translated into Mandarin.

Although my speech was only a few minutes long, I felt that I needed to express our appreciation for this opportunity to play a small part in the growth of China. The Bishop Estate, I stressed, was not the usual white, Anglo-Saxon, Protestant American group. All of the trustees were *keiko o ka aina*— children of the land of Hawai'i who could trace their roots back to Asia. We were from Hawai'i, a multiracial and multi-cultural society, and were therefore sensitive to their concerns beyond economics.

As I stood in this esteemed place, I could not help but reflect on how this *keiki o ka aina,* born of humble origins, had personally come to this point in the history of China, Hawai'i, and the Bishop Estate. At such defining moments in the passage of a lifetime, the people, places, and events that influence our lives assume new importance. The tapestry of the past that shaped me suddenly seemed a vibrant patchwork of memories stretching across seven decades of plantation life, war, evolution, and emergence.

CHAPTER ONE

From Hawai'i's Plantation to Europe's Battleground

THE HAWAI'I IN which I was born in the 1920s would be a foreign world to the modern generation of islanders familiar with the bustling cosmopolitan society of the Hawaiian Islands. I grew up in Haleiwa, a small town on the North Shore of Oahu, which was at the time a tight-knit community primarily consisting of Japanese and a few Hawaiian and Chinese families. The area was surrounded by small plantation villages in Waialua, where first-generation Japanese, Korean, Portuguese, and Filipino immigrant sugar laborers and their families struggled to survive within a contract labor system— a system that exploited immigrants to establish a highly profitable sugar industry. This was a Hawai'i where multiethnic languages and customs were commonplace and the racial restrictions of place and color were taken for granted.

My parents were Japanese immigrants who joined the tens of thousands of other foreign laborers seeking a better life for themselves and their children in an alien world. My father came to Hawai'i from Kagawa Prefecture on the island of Shikoku, a place that produced few emigrants to Hawai'i. After his first wife died, leaving him to care for two sons alone, he left Japan. Since he was in debt, he thought that going to Hawai'i would provide a fresh start. Once in Hawai'i, my father married his second wife, my mother, who had also been widowed. Her first marriage was to a man named Nonaka, with whom she had several sons and daughters.

My mother played a major role in my life because of her strong belief in education. My father, on the other hand, was more interested in seeing his sons get jobs as soon as it was legally possible for them to quit school. He became seriously ill and returned to Japan when I was a sophomore in high school. My mother was then free to encourage me to continue my education. After attending Waialua Elementary and Andrew E. Cox Intermediate Schools, I graduated in 1940 at the age of seventeen in the second graduating class of Waialua High School.

At the time, most of the students who attended the high school were nisei, although there were some Chinese, Filipino, and Korean children from plantation camps in the Waialua district. Everyone knew everyone else, and doors were never locked. Growing up with that kind of common ethnic background and culture in a rural area encouraged close and lasting friendships.

There was some comfort and security in knowing one's place in an established plantation world, where the positions of white management and immigrant workers were clearly delineated. Even in my youth, however, I had aspirations beyond the life of Waialua. I served as the editor of the school paper, vice president of the student body in my junior year, and president in my senior year. This helped heighten my ambitions. Winning student body elections was not that difficult since my class consisted of only about ninety students, all of whom I knew. The high school had no more than three hundred students. In fact, during my election campaign for vice president and later president, I was the only candidate.

While these early "political" experiences were only student government elections in a small rural high school, they made adjustment to my later political career much easier. When the ILWU left me off their list of endorsements during my first campaign for election to the Honolulu Board of Supervisors in 1952, many of my former classmates and wartime buddies, then active union members in Waialua, objected long and hard. I was eventually added to the ILWU list and endorsed.

Among the teachers who influenced me and encouraged me always to reach beyond the life of the sugar plantation were our high school principal, William Geiger, and teachers like Barbara Clopton, Albert Tyau, and Hanako Miyamoto. Bill Geiger was a caring person who encouraged me to participate actively in student government. Teachers like Mrs. Clopton and Mrs. Miyamoto took a special interest in my academic training. They, along with Albert Tyau, encouraged me to go to the University of Hawai'i, and to Teachers College in particular. They taught me to speak standard English, helped me polish my speeches as a student leader in high school, and corrected my use of written and oral English. I can still remember a faux pas I made while introducing a speaker at a student assembly. Wanting to show how smart I was, I delivered a memorized introduction, which described the guest speaker as an "imminent" scholar. I did not know at that time that the correct term was "eminent." The students were not aware of the difference, but the teachers and the speaker caught my error. I never forgot the embarrassment of that day and thereafter learned to check meanings of words before I used them.

My first job was on the sugar plantation. Like almost every fifteen-year-old high school student in Waialua, I worked on the plantation during the summer. Our *luna*, or overseers, were usually our teachers. Since we were unskilled, we weeded with hoes—menial, backbreaking work for which we were paid not by the hour but by the number of lines of cane we weeded. Minimum wage was unheard of at that time, so my first earnings for a full day's work was only 18 cents. I was not good at this kind of work. When we returned to the same field for the same rate the next day, I rebelled and walked home. My parents were told by the teacher-*luna* that I had been a "bad boy." Needless to say, after being reprimanded by my parents, I went back to work the next day.

In those days plantation work was the only paying job available to teenagers in Waialua. Eventually, the price per line for weeding and my skill both improved. During the next summer some of us were promoted to *hanawai*, or irrigation work, for which we were paid $1.25—a considerable raise! In addition, the work was much easier. The following summers I worked in the pineapple fields, where the pay was even better. The drawback, however, was that I had to live in a pineapple camp for the summer, where workers were housed and fed. The work was much more hazardous since we were using knives to cut off the tops of pineapples. I still bear a scar from the day I missed a pineapple top and nearly cut off my left thumb.

The first paycheck (for more than fifteen days' work) I received from Waialua Sugar Company was for a little over $17. As was the custom among the Japanese families in those days, I gave all the money to my mother. She gave me a little spending money, but the rest went toward family expenses. Everyone in my family was busy working, earning a living, and contributing to a common fund just so that we could survive as a family. My mother held the purse strings. Like most other families, despite our collective efforts we remained poor. During most of my early years, I went to school barefoot or wearing slippers; I did not get my first pair of canvas tennis shoes until I attended intermediate school.

My father was a trucker who delivered rice, canned goods, and other merchandise from Honolulu wholesalers to Waialua retailers. As his son, I was expected to help him out every day after finishing Japanese language school. He would pick me up at a prearranged location, and I assisted him by carrying cases of canned goods and bags of rice from the truck to the retail store. Working for my father was a family obligation, so I received no pay. I occasionally rebelled, running off to play with my schoolmates, but when I returned home there would always be hell to pay. The next day I would be back at work. My memories of my father are perhaps most vivid when I recall how I was sent by my mother to the neighbors' houses, where he was gambling (playing *hanafuda,* a Japanese card game) and drinking with friends, to tell him it was time to come home for dinner.

When I was fourteen years old, my father became partially paralyzed because of cerebral thrombosis and could no longer run his business. My brother, who was working at the army PX, took over the trucking business. One of my father's sons in Japan, a half brother whom I never met, wanted my father to return to Osaka, where they could take care of him. I think the thought of returning to Japan appealed to him, so he left Hawai'i, never to return. I never saw my father again. Just before the outbreak of World War II, he passed away in Osaka, Japan.

While much of my Japanese language and values were passed on to me by my parents, Japanese language school also played a major role. Children of immigrant Japanese families were required to attend Japanese language school after English school from first grade through high school. Our language school was held at the Buddhist church in Haleiwa. In addition to learning how to read and write Japanese, we also studied Japanese history and *shushin,* or the study of ethics. In the evenings, I studied judo with a *sensei,* or teacher, from Japan. Through language school I gained some understanding and knowledge of the Japanese language and culture. During those years, I got to know the Reverend Buntetsu Miyamoto of the church, who later became the bishop of the Jodo Mission. He remained one of my friends until he passed away.

The nisei who grew up on the plantations of Hawai'i shared a common struggle for economic survival and suffered from the same racial and social biases. The language schools and our parents instilled a strong sense of Japanese values of duty, loyalty, and filial piety. Although I paid less and less attention to my Japanese studies as I got older, the schools and my parents had successfully instilled in me the importance of *shushin.* These values were reinforced in the American schools, where the lives of Abraham Lincoln and George Washington were presented to us as American role models. With daily lessons in *giri,* or obligation and duty, it is little wonder that my generation placed such importance on the value of loyalty and obligation to country, community, family, and friends. Bringing shame to one's family was seen as an unpardonable sin. Knowing who one's real friends were and always being willing to help them in times of need were abiding values I learned and inherited and now wish to teach to my children and grandchildren.

As student body vice president and president of Waialua High School, I was able to attend public high school conferences on the neighboring islands. During these meetings, I associated with students from all of the public high schools, broadening my contacts with other student leaders throughout the islands. Many of us shared the common ambition of our Asian immigrant parents to become teachers. This was the only realistic goal, since graduate professional school was out of financial reach and most professional occupations were restricted to *haoles.*

The first step to becoming a teacher was to study at the University of Hawaiʻi's Teachers College. Only a few of the brightest candidates were accepted. I was the only student in my graduating class from Waialua High School to be admitted. At Teachers College I met many friends whom I had originally come to know at the conferences, such as Shiro Amioka of McKinley High School, who later became superintendent of the Department of Education of Hawaiʻi. Attending Teachers College seemed like old home week for many of us, and our friendships helped us make the transition from high school to college.

I moved to Honolulu in the summer of 1940 to attend the University of Hawaiʻi. Since I was the first one in my family to go to college, my half brothers and sisters encouraged me and were a great help. I stayed with my half sister, Leatrice, and her family and worked as a dishwasher during the summer for $45 a month at Charlie's Place, a restaurant on Pauahi Street owned by my brother-in-law. The rest of my family helped by providing me with spending money. When I entered Teachers College that fall, I was leading a simple, subsistence life typical of a relatively poor student from a small, rural town.

After one semester in college, I was invited to join an elite group of male students in what became known as the Wentworth Rohr Group. Wentworth Rohr, an instructor at Teachers

College during the 1940s, gathered about twenty male students who had attained a B or better grade point average and
shepherded them through the college curriculum. I was doing
well in my studies after completing my first year at Teachers
College. I decided, however, that I wanted to go beyond teaching to some other profession, as yet undetermined. I knew that
to reach that goal I would need a nest egg for future schooling.
With this in mind, I decided to apply for a full-time job as a
civilian clerk, a position that was available with the United
States Army at Fort Armstrong, located near downtown Honolulu. Starting with what was considered at that time a good
wage of 50 cents an hour, I got a job that required me to be on
the base during the day. I attended night school at the University of Hawai'i, carrying as many credits as I could so I could
continue my education. Being separated from my high school
classmates and without any real close friends in the city, I
drudged along working and studying until that fateful day
when life in Hawai'i would be dramatically changed.

Before the attack on Pearl Harbor on December 7, 1941, my
nisei friends and I really did not think very much about Japan.
Many of us were dual citizens—American citizens by birth
and Japanese citizens through blood and parentage. The dual
citizenship issue was esoteric to us in high school. The relationship between the United States and Japan in world affairs
was of little concern to us. Nothing really changed for us as a
result of Japan's aggression in China—something taking place
in another part of the world very distant from rural Hawai'i.
For us, Japan was simply the home of our parents.

Even as the bellicose rhetoric and hostility between Japan
and the United States heightened, few of us took the situation
seriously. The name-calling reports were meaningless words
of politicians. We did not believe that war would ever occur.
Perhaps because I was working for the United States Army at
Fort Armstrong, I was even more convinced than others that
the rhetoric would not signal a real conflict between Japan
and the United States. Many of the nisei and other non-white
locals employed at the fort continued to work as they had

always done, taking care of the carpentry, plumbing, and electrical problems of the military base. No one ever questioned us or associated us with the Japanese in Japan. The morning of December 7, 1941, suddenly revealed to us how naive we had been in believing that a war could "never happen here."

On Saturday afternoon, December 6, the University of Hawai'i football team played Willamette College at Honolulu Stadium. The University of Hawai'i team trounced the mainland team 20–6. With hundreds of other students I attended an after-game evening dance at Hemenway Hall on campus. I took my date home after midnight, returned to my sister's place in McCully, and finally fell asleep about 2:00 A.M. My sister woke me up at 8:00 that morning, telling me that an announcement on the radio said that Japanese planes were attacking Pearl Harbor. "Forget it," I sleepily told her. "It's only an army and navy maneuver at Pearl Harbor." Like many other civilians that morning, we could not believe that something like this would happen. There had to be another explanation.

As we slowly realized what was really happening, we were dumbstruck by the audacity of Japan in attacking Pearl Harbor. Urgent messages were broadcast over the radio to military personnel and employees of military installations to report to work immediately. I reported to my office at Fort Armstrong, where we were put on standby to help as ordered by the military officers. Although the base and the surrounding areas were untouched by the bombing, there was incredible confusion for a few days as we stayed on standby duty. As civilian workers of Japanese ancestry, the status of the nisei on the base did not change. Since Fort Armstrong was a housekeeping base and not high security, those of us who were nisei continued to work as we did before.

The situation for young Japanese Americans working on the military base in militarily sensitive capacities was quite different. Immediately after the attack on Pearl Harbor, all full-time day students, including nisei, who were enrolled in ROTC at the University of Hawai'i were called to report to the Territorial Guard for military duty. The nisei, however, were dismissed from duty soon thereafter, their loyalty to the United States now doubted by the military commanders. Wanting to demonstrate their loyalty by helping in the war effort after their dismissal, these nisei students started the Varsity Victory Volunteers (VVV), a civilian defense group affiliated with the army to engage in a variety of noncombat wartime activities. I had many friends in the VVV and I wanted to join them. I tried to resign from my position at Fort Armstrong, but the authorities at the fort refused my request because I was considered an essential defense worker.

In January 1942, I enrolled as a full-time student at the University of Hawai'i since this was the only way I could resign from working at Fort Armstrong. To earn some money to pay for my schooling, I worked at my older half brother's jewelry shop on Union Street. During the critical first months of the war, I became close to Dr. Shunzo Sakamaki, a university professor who was very active in the nisei morale group, which coordinated communication between the Japanese community and the military. This group was mostly comprised of new leaders in the Japanese community, older nisei professionals who took charge after the former issei leaders had become suspect aliens. At the time, the nisei could not enlist for military service. All of us were classified by the Selective Service as "IV-C," not acceptable for service for reasons of ancestry. However, a few hundred nisei who had been drafted into the United States Army prior to the attack on Pearl Harbor were still in the military. They had been reorganized and trained as a single all-nisei unit, the 100th Infantry Battalion designated to serve in Europe. After receiving a good training record in Camp McCoy, Wisconsin, the 100th Battalion was prepared to go into combat. The 100th's excellent training record and the unblemished record of the VVV, which did essential civil defense work on Oahu, intensified our effort to allow Japanese Americans to volunteer for military combat service. Many organized groups such as the morale committee pressed the government to allow us to demonstrate our loyalty in combat. Finally, President Franklin D. Roosevelt signed a proclamation in March 1943 authorizing the formation of an all-nisei volunteer unit, the 442nd Regimental Combat Team, to serve in combat in the European theater. This was the chance we had been waiting for.

Realizing that the nisei of Hawai'i had to respond positively to this call for volunteers, Shunzo Sakamaki asked that I join four other nisei students in going around the island, talking to groups of young Japanese Americans about how important it was that we answer this challenge. We told them that the stakes were very high for us. Over and over we spoke to groups of young nisei, stressing that this was our chance to show our loyalty to our country, to demonstrate to the people of this country where our hearts were. We could not let our critics say that because we were of Japanese ancestry and our enemy was Japan, we would not fight for our country. Although this message was very simple, we could not risk failure. Our actions, we knew, would determine the future of our families, our generation, and the future generations of Japanese Americans in Hawai'i.

One advantage that this recruiting role gave me was that I had all the gas ration coupons I needed to do this "essential work." I was driving all over town and the rural areas whenever and wherever I was needed to speak to an interested group of young nisei. Although many of these young men were deeply hurt by the mistrust shown to them by their country of birth, I was very encouraged by their response wherever I went. They understood the circumstances and reasons for the highly charged emotions against Japan, the country of our parents, and wanted to show their commitment to America. Issei were also volunteering in the war effort by joining the Keawe Corps or buying war bonds. Almost everyone we knew, issei and nisei, was trying to demonstrate loyalty to the United States.

Not once in all those weeks did I encounter anyone who challenged me as a lackey of the United States or the military government. Whether it was fair or not, we knew we had to prove that we were as loyal as any white American. I knew of cases of mistreatment of families by the military. Fathers were suddenly taken out of their homes, with no evidence of having committed any crime, and were imprisoned at Schofield Barracks.

Once we all enlisted, we were later taken by train to the Oahu Land and Railway Company station near Aala Park and marched to board the *Lurline,* the famous passenger liner that traveled between Hawai'i and the West Coast. The *Lurline* had been refitted as a troop transport. We sailed to Oakland, California, where we boarded a train that had all the window shades pulled down. Many of us were not sure why this had been done, but guessed that we were being shielded from public view in California, where all persons of Japanese ancestry, U.S. citizens or not, had been shipped to internment centers. My most vivid memory of the train trip across the country was going through the Sierra Nevada mountains in March when the snow was still falling. Because this was the first time most of us had ever seen snow, they stopped the train to let us off. We jumped around in the snow like a bunch of kids. This was also the first time most of us had ever been to the mainland— many of the boys had not even traveled to the neighbor islands. Sailing from Honolulu to Oakland on the *Lurline* and going across the mainland on a train was for many of us a great adventure.

The train eventually took us to Camp Shelby near Hattiesburg, Mississippi. Upon arrival, I remember seeing an article in one of the local papers quoting a Mississippi congressman who was referring to the "Jap invasion of Mississippi." I had almost finished the article before I realized that he was talking about us. It was a little unsettling to realize that I was considered a Japanese enemy in the heartland of America. The army was also concerned about the potentially explosive situation caused by our presence in the South. Not long after we settled into camp, the entire regiment was assembled by the regimental commander. "This is a racially segregated society," the colonel explained to us. "Remember, you are considered white. You are not to go into the colored bathrooms or public areas designated for the colored. You're supposed to go on the white side. While you are here, you are considered white."

Our first reaction to this announcement was disbelief. Then we were relieved. Many of us thought that we would probably be better off on the white side than on the "colored" side. The racial implications of this segregationist policy did not strike us until we got a good taste of southern society. On one occasion we were riding a bus to Hattiesburg. The front of the bus designated for whites was full, with people standing. Yet the back of the bus set aside for "coloreds" was completely empty. Some of the nisei men went into that colored section and sat down. The driver stopped the bus and yelled at them to get out of that section. They had to move into the white section even though they had to stand up in the aisle. This happened many times, and the absurdity of the situation became more and more apparent. On one occasion, some of our men got so mad at the driver they took him off the bus and beat him up.

There were other kinds of racial problems. One evening I even got thrown into the stockade over a racial slur. Three of us had been out that night eating watermelon when we saw one of the 442nd men in trouble with a *haole* from the 69th Division who had called him a "Jap." We did not know who this Japanese American was, but it did not matter. He had a red band on his hat, which meant he was in our artillery. All of us, especially those of us from Hawai'i, felt that if any member of the 442nd got into a fight, we had to help—no questions asked. Even though we were generally smaller in physical stature than the white soldier or civilian, we had the advantage of immediate collective support from other members of the unit. So we jumped into this scrap to help. The MPs arrested us, and we were all locked up in the stockade for the night.

After a few of these fights, the white soldiers soon learned that we were not going to take insults or abuse from anybody. And "Jap" was clearly a fighting word. I was told later by a white soldier whom I befriended in the hospital that the white soldiers had been told by the inspector general never to call us

"Japs." If you do, they were warned, there would be a fight. And they knew this was true from experience.

As we learned more about our new environment, we saw other differences between life on the mainland and life in Hawai'i. Most strikingly, for the first time we saw Caucasians as common workers, even serving as waitresses and salesclerks. They were not supervisors and managers telling us what to do. In Hawai'i, the whites were always on a tier above us, ordering us to work. Some of us experienced mild culture shock. After this mainland experience, I knew Hawai'i would never be the same. None of us who would return to Hawai'i would again accept second-class status.

One of the unsettling questions we continued to face during training camp was whether we would serve in combat as a unit. Most of us believed that to prove our loyalty beyond a doubt, we needed to distinguish ourselves in combat. We had to prove that we were as good as, if not better than, any other fighting American unit. Although no one really said it openly, this driving force to prove ourselves was evident. At one of our company meetings we were asked by a white officer why we had volunteered to join the 442nd. We told him simply that we needed to prove to our country that we were Americans. We were not Japanese. We were Japanese Americans fighting for the United States.

Although infantry training in camp was tough, we were young and got in shape quickly. One thing that made us different from other units at Camp Shelby was the number of showers we took. The white soldiers saw us coming back from the field for a short lunch hour; instead of eating and relaxing, many of us showered. Then we would put our uniforms back on, eat a quick lunch, and return to training. At the end of the day, we would take another shower. Even though our water bill must have been very high, our cleanliness impressed the white officers, who did not realize that our Japanese cultural background demanded we take daily baths.

The food in the army also took a little adjustment since they usually served us potatoes instead of rice. Eventually, they did try to accommodate our diet by serving rice. Earl Finch, one of the residents of Hattiesburg who adopted the 442nd and became our good friend, also tried to help us feel less homesick. He used to have fresh red snapper delivered to us from New Orleans so that we could have sashimi.

Whenever we got down to New Orleans on a pass, we made a ritual out of eating sashimi for dinner at a traditional American restaurant. First, we'd have lunch at a Chinese restaurant, where we would buy a bottle of shoyu. Then we'd go to a regular restaurant that had seafood on the menu. Most restaurants served snapper because that was a common variety of fish in that region. We told the waiter to tell the chef how we wanted the fresh snapper prepared: fillet the fish as is and slice it; place the raw, fresh slices on a plate of shredded lettuce or cabbage; and bring it out to us as an appetizer. We also asked him to get some yellow mustard and to mix it with hot water into a paste, and to bring it out with the sliced raw fish. We would then mix the shoyu we bought from the Chinese restaurant with the mustard and eat the sliced raw red snapper on shredded lettuce, dipping it in the shoyu mixture. These waiters must have thought we were cannibals! At the time sashimi was rarely served on the mainland. Not only was the red snapper very good, but we had a great time confusing and shocking the waiters.

On one of my early three-day passes to Chicago, I met Ayako Saiki, my future wife, in a small hotel in which we were both staying. Aya, as she was known, was the youngest of four sisters and a brother who had grown up in Southern California. At the outbreak of the war, her college education was interrupted as she and her family were removed from their home and placed in the horse stables at Santa Anita race track until they were transferred and incarcerated at the Rohwer, Arkansas, internment camp. After the War Relocation Authority decided to allow internees to leave the camps for employment outside the West Coast area, she found work as a civilian clerk at Fort Sheridan, Illinois.

When I first saw her, she and her sister were waiting for someone they knew from the army. Apparently their signals got crossed and they were left waiting in the lobby. My friend and I ended up filling in for the evening. After we had dinner together, they returned to Fort Sheridan, but not before we exchanged addresses. We started to correspond with each other, and whenever I had the chance, I went to Chicago from Camp Shelby to meet her. She sent me care packages in camp. I was one of the lucky ones from Hawai'i who received these food packages in camp, overseas, and on my return to the United States from a caring mainland connection.

As our training came to an end, we began to prepare for combat. The 442nd Regimental Combat Team was composed of a regiment of three rifle battalions and support units, a battalion of artillery, and a company of engineers. At Camp Shelby, I was in C Company, First Battalion. When we were training in army maneuvers, we participated as a whole unit. However, when the 442nd was ready to go overseas in May 1944, the First Battalion was broken up to provide replacement reserves for the Second, Third, and 100th Battalions; subsequently the 100th Battalion became the First Battalion of the regiment. I was in a group of non-coms from the First Battalion who were held back as cadre for training future replacements for the 442nd.

Those of us left behind at Camp Shelby were reorganized as the 171st Battalion and were engaged in training the new replacements for the 442nd. While waiting for the draftees to gather together, four of us were assigned to a special detached service to make an army training film in June 1944. We were sent to Vero Beach, Florida, to serve under a colonel who had been at Schofield Barracks. He was assigned as a military advisor to make an army training film for soldiers who would go into combat in the South Pacific. One of the cameramen was Red Skelton's brother. The four of us with Japanese faces were the Japanese enemy in the film; we were dressed up in Japanese Imperial Army uniforms and instructed how to act as enemy soldiers. In the next few days I was killed first on the beach at Vero Beach; then I was shot down in the ocean; I was finally blown up in the jungles of Silver Springs, Florida. This was my most enjoyable army assignment. During the thirty days of filming, we lived in a hotel and were given first-class civilian service. I never saw the training film, but they told us it was quite good.

Soon after my only filmmaking experience, the army called for trained replacements for the 442nd in Europe. Many of us who had been left behind from the original 442nd wanted to join them. We asked to go with the replacements we had trained, and I was one of the NCOs selected to go overseas. As replacements, we were all assigned to various companies that needed men to fill the void caused by the casualties of combat. I ended up in L Company, joining the unit in Epinal, France. I was fortunate. The bloody battle of Vosges forest, including the rescue of the lost battalion of the 36th Texas Division, had already taken place. As a result, the 442nd had been badly decimated and had pulled back to Epinal to rebuild with replacements. From Epinal we came down to southern France along the French-Italian border, staying in the mountains bordering France and Italy, holding and defending the line as more replacements came in to bring the unit back up to full strength again. My first taste of combat was relatively mild, with only occasional enemy shelling and skirmishes. There was very little fighting in this holding action. The Germans and Americans were facing each other across the mountains defending the French-Italian border.

When we got a three-day pass we went to Nice, a city on the French Riviera, for rest and recreation. The local money, such as the French franc, was of little value. Chocolate bars were of far greater value, and cigarettes were even more valuable than chocolates. Since nylon stockings were in great demand back home, we bartered for them by trading our cigarettes. Perfumes were next in priority. I sent Aya whatever stockings and perfumes I could barter for from the French. She continued to send me care packages from Chicago. Letters from her and home were also a real treat. All of us wrote as frequently as we could to our girlfriends and families back in the islands. Since my mother never understood or wrote English and I could not write in Japanese, I kept in touch with her through my brothers and sisters, who let her know how I was doing.

Vivid memories of my experiences in the war zone remain with me a half century later. Food and clothing were scarce for the civilians who were trying to survive as best as they could. We felt the most sorry for the children, who often hung around the mess area watching us eat with silent eyes. We gave them whatever we could. This memory of hungry children is a lasting one that reminds me of the high price war extracts from its innocent victims.

I can still remember how I felt whenever we were told that we were going to cross the line into combat. Many of us had a sinking feeling that we might not be as lucky as the last time, when we came out whole. We were scared, but we did not want to show it. We spent the night before drinking any alcohol we could get. It was dumb and irrational to get drunk and try to forget what lay ahead in combat. Yet the gnawing sense of not knowing what was going to happen left us with an empty feeling. Circumstances were beyond our control, but we found strength in knowing that we were not alone. So long as we were together under fire, we could count on the support and loyalty of our friends. In these hours of free time before going into combat, we drank, we gambled, and we lived from one moment to the next.

A regimental combat team like the 442nd is large, with three infantry battalions and supporting units, like anti-tank service, cannon groups, a battalion of field artillery, and a company of engineers. An infantry battalion has four companies: three rifle and one heavy weapons company. L Company was one of the four companies of the Third Battalion. Each company had three rifle platoons, one weapons platoon, and supporting administrative and service units. I was in the weapons platoon, which had two sections—a machine gun unit and a mortar unit. I was in the mortar squad.

The men in the rifle platoon were on the first line in combat and the weapons platoon with machine guns and mortars supported them. The three line companies of the infantry battalion were supported by the heavy weapons company, with heavier and larger-caliber machine guns and mortars. Behind the infantry battalions was the 522nd Artillery Battalion, with heavy artillery to support the infantry battalions. The company of engineers naturally dealt with all the engineering problems of the regimental combat team. The 522nd Artillery Battalion did not return with the 442nd Regiment from southern France to northern France for the final push up the Italian peninsula. They joined other American units to invade Germany and were among those who liberated concentration camp victims at Dachau.

After the 442nd finally got up to full strength again, we went from southern France to northern Italy. We were attached to the 92nd Division, an African American division, and assigned to face the entrenched German forces in the Apennines Mountains. Because they controlled the high peaks, the Germans could observe all movements from the mountains to the sea. The highest peak of this mountain range was Mount Folgorito, located miles away from the coastal plain. One side of the mountain was narrow and steep, without regular trails, and was considered unassailable by the Germans, who had fixed their guns defensively on the more accessible slopes of the mountain, rising from the coastal plains toward their defensive position in the heights. The 100th Battalion was assigned the task of attacking the German defensive position from the coastal plains upward. The Third Battalion was ordered to climb the slopes to Mount Folgorito and attack the enemy from the rear.

We quietly moved into position at dusk, preparing to cross the line of departure at the base of Mount Folgorito at 6:00 P.M. We were to climb single file up the steep slope of the mountain. We climbed all night, reaching the top at 6:00 A.M. The 100th Battalion attacked the same morning, coming up from the coastal plain and assaulting the entrenched German position. The Second Battalion was to be in reserve. We reached the top on time as planned, and completely surprised the Germans. We moved quickly down the mountain to meet the 100th Battalion, which was facing increasing fire from the German fortifications. The 100th, however, kept unrelenting pressure on the Germans and sustained substantial casualties. The German defensive line collapsed that day as a result of the unexpected attack from the rear, which was exposed and defenseless. The pincer movement of the 100th and Third Battalions succeeded in breaching the German defensive position, and the 442nd earned another presidential citation.

In the 442nd, we met friends we had known in high school and at the university who were in other companies. We bumped into each other in camp, on passes in Hattiesburg and New Orleans, on furloughs in Chicago and New York, and overseas in the most unexpected places, such as a street corner of Dijon, France. For instance, on an overnight layover from Epinal to Nice, I unexpectedly met an old friend from college who was in E Company. But even if we were strangers, we became instant friends as long as we wore the 442nd patch. The bond forged among nisei veterans of the 442nd or 100th was special. We walked the same road; we had the same goal; we carried the hopes and aspirations of our family and community to one day proudly proclaim our heritage justified by our record in combat. Our honor was earned under fire.

Lessons are learned quickly on the front line. Avoid trees when choosing a site for a foxhole—artillery bursting on a tree and showering shrapnel can be devastating to those in an uncovered foxhole. A reverse slope is safe from artillery fire since the projectile has a known trajectory. However, this position is not as safe from a mortar shell, which has a trajectory different from that of artillery. A mortar shell can come almost straight down after reaching its highest level, so the reverse slope may not be safe. One learns from these lessons to survive.

The mind is a wonderful thing that can forget, or push into the deepest recesses of the brain, the unpleasant and difficult experiences of the past. The feelings of fear, fatigue, hunger, frustration, and hurt suffered during war do not continue throughout life. Only with effort can I now recall my unpleasant past experiences. I can talk about the war, but I no longer really feel it. I can, however, still vividly recall the frightening experience we had when we entered the marble town of

Carrara. We entered from the mountains, and the Germans zeroed in on us with their big naval guns from the coastal city of La Spezia. The sound of huge shells exploding on the stones of the town near us was deafening. We huddled in the stone buildings until the shelling was over, and then pulled out of town in a hurry, returning to the safety of mountainside.

Milan was a more enjoyable experience. We came out of the mountains and found streetcars waiting to take us into town. Tired and dirty, we were given quarters in the vacated town buildings. After we had settled in, we went looking for a large *furo*. We had heard about Roman bathhouses and eventually found one. We washed ourselves and soaked in a warm bath, enjoying that deeply wonderful sense of being clean again.

As far as I knew, I never shot or killed anyone. I fired my carbine in the direction of the enemy line, but never directly at a person. I was a lousy shot anyway. I did not have much of a reaction when I first saw corpses of enemy soldiers. However, it was different whenever I saw someone from our own units. I could not erase the thought that this could have been me. Since I identified with every one of our men, the sight of these corpses was something that always affected me. This is one reason why, to this day, I do not want to have anything to do with guns.

Although I was exposed to enemy fire, I was fortunate never to have been wounded. I keep telling people that I always dug a good slit trench. In one instance, a nearby mortar burst and sent shrapnel in a direction away from where I was lying. A soldier on the other side, farther away from the burst, was hit. There were a few incidents when I escaped injury while others were not as fortunate. After a few of these experiences, I developed a fatalistic attitude. If it is going to happen, it will happen. My fate is out of my control. This attitude made life more bearable.

Another way many of us kept our nerves in combat was to tell ourselves that we could not bring shame to ourselves, our parents, and our company. There was a certain amount of pride in being a "buddhahead." This fear of "making shame" was a pillar of strength in combat. I never saw anyone run away during combat. There was no question that everybody was scared, but we always felt that we had to prove ourselves to be good combat soldiers.

This fear of bringing shame had been driven into us by our parents and the Japanese language school. Our role models emphasized that courage and compassion in a warrior would bring credit to family and community. Heroic films such as *Chūshingura: The Forty-Seven Ronin*, instilled in us a certain perception of pride and loyalty. In Camp Shelby we used to drink beer and sing Japanese military marching songs. *Yamato Damashi*, a slogan that extolled the pride and spirit of the Japanese soldier, reminded us of who we were. This spirit of old Japan was being extolled by the 442nd Regiment, fighting to prove its loyalty to the United States. If the nisei were outstanding soldiers, our valor could be largely attributed to these basic Japanese values.

When the 442nd got to Europe, the 100th Battalion already had earned an enviable reputation as the "Purple Heart Battalion" for their bravery under fire. The military newspaper, *Stars and Stripes*, started to publicize the exploits of the 442nd and 100th in Italy and France. Our unit was also starting to receive citations, and General Mark Clark was saying what great soldiers we were. While we were aware of our reputation, we never really thought of ourselves as an elite unit. We did what we did because we knew we had to do it; the loyalty of our generation was in question. Trying to be the best was more important than just being brave.

We were also aware that the army was sending us where we were most needed. Often we were placed in some of the most difficult lead positions, such as the time we were assigned to help the 92nd Division break through a strongly established German line in the Apennines Mountains. The rescue of the First Battalion, 141st Infantry Regiment of the 36th Division was another example of the unit's willingness to "go for broke." At that time the 442nd was supposed to be in reserve, but it was called by the division commander to penetrate the

German lines surrounding the lost battalion and rescue them. Proud of our record, we never questioned the orders given to us, but did as we were told. The price we paid to prove our loyalty, in blood, was high.

By 1945, the Germans had become weak. During our final push in northern Italy, there were no German airplanes. The stubby American P47s gave us air support, unopposed by enemy fighters. We knew that it was only a question of time before the Germans would be defeated. There was no question we were going to win Italy.

After VE day, I stayed with the unit below the Swiss border to process German prisoners. At that time the army was looking for volunteers to serve as Japanese language interpreters in the South Pacific. Although I knew I would be taking risks if I volunteered, I wanted to get back to the United States and Hawai'i as quickly as possible. The interpreters school was located in Minneapolis, which was close to Chicago where Aya worked. My younger brother was also at the interpreters school. He had just been drafted to be trained as an interpreter to serve in the Pacific theater. I calculated that I had enough points to be discharged from the service, so I volunteered again, and was flown from Italy to Casablanca, then to Brazil, Puerto Rico, Florida, and finally Chicago. On VJ day, August 14, 1945, I was in Minneapolis starting my schooling to become an interpreter. When the news reached us that Japan had unconditionally surrendered, I felt a deep sense of relief that World War II was finally over and looked forward to starting a new life as a civilian.

When I finally returned to Hawai'i, there were no flags waving, no ceremonies, no cheering crowds. The reunion with my mother and family was joyous, but very private and quiet. Spark Matsunaga, who was then an officer of the 100th Battalion, tried to get me to join the Army Reserve, but I refused. I received my discharge from the army in November 1945 at Fort Kamehameha, near Honolulu.

I do not know whether I was different by the time the war ended. Nearly four years had passed from the start to the end of World War II, an interlude in which the status of the nisei changed. The experience gave the nisei the basis for saying, "Look, I proved that I'm as good as anybody else in this country. I can demand equal opportunity, an equal chance." The war had served as a proving ground and starting point. When we came back, the old plantation system was still in place, but it was changing because of the labor union movement. Many of us were no longer willing to accept the same system. We wanted to change the way things were in Hawai'i. In fact, I admit that some of us had some real big chips on our shoulders. We were young, emotional, and more confrontational than our older nisei peers who had not gone to war. With the GI Bill of Rights we were able to attend graduate and professional schools. We were not revolutionaries. Nor were we trying to overturn the whole society. Willing to play by the rules of the game, we knew what changes we wanted to initiate and how we could possibly achieve them. With little money, we were also aware of our social and economic limitations. Yet we had the numbers, we had the education, and we had the intelligence and motivation to challenge the existing system. We were ready for a change.

CHAPTER TWO

Hawai'i after the War: A Time for Change

EVEN AFTER THE war, the nisei's desire to prove themselves as first-class Americans continued to be a driving force. Our military service qualified us to receive certain benefits under the GI Bill of Rights. For those of us whose university careers had been suspended by war service, this was a godsend, providing us with financial support to resume our college education. Going to excellent universities on the mainland was no longer an impossible dream, and we took this opportunity to pursue the very best education possible.

Since Aya was still working in Chicago, I decided to use my GI stipend to enroll in a university in that area and pursue a professional education. In December 1945, I boarded a war administration ship that sailed from Honolulu to San Francisco. There were about five of us from the 442nd on the ship. To pass time on board, I played table stake poker with mainland GIs who had just gotten their severance pay. The stakes became pretty high. At first I just watched. After about a day, I noticed there was only one pro. Except for him, the other GIs were playing like it was a $2-limit game. Since I used to play a lot of table stake poker in the 442nd, I decided to join the game using as my table stake the several hundred dollars in cash I was carrying. By the time we got to San Francisco, the pro and I had won most of the money. I felt so sorry for one guy who lost and was completely broke that I gave him enough money to get home. With all the cash I won I tried to

47

catch a plane to Chicago, but none were available. Consequently, I ended up going all the way across the country on
one of those slow trains that seemed to stop at every town. I
joined Aya in Evanston, Illinois, and with my University of
Hawai'i transcripts in hand, I applied to the business school at
Northwestern University and the law school at the University of Chicago. Fortunately, the law school at the University
of Chicago allowed a qualified student with at least two years
of university credit to apply for a special four-year program
rather than the normal three-year program. Through this program I was able to enter law school without having to obtain
a bachelor's degree first.

One of the questions on the application to law school asked
my reason for applying. Besides stating generally that I wanted
to be an attorney, I specifically wrote that one of the things I
really wanted to find out was the constitutionality of the internment of citizens of Japanese ancestry during the war. I was
probably the only one among all the applicants who had raised
a question about this very real constitutional issue. Although
I did not hear from Northwestern University, I was accepted
by the University of Chicago law school.

The law school used a quarter system, so I started my four-
year program in the spring quarter in March 1946 as the only
nisei in the whole school. There was only one other person of
Asian ancestry, a student from China who had graduated from
a Chinese university before he immigrated to the United
States. There were also five African Americans in our class. I
was sort of an oddity, being a Japanese American from Hawai'i. I remained the only nisei in the class until the quarter
before I graduated, when Patsy Takemoto Mink and Edward
Nakamura entered the law school.

Of our entering class, about ten of us were in the four-year
program while the others were college graduates in the traditional three-year program. Since we had to complete four
years, we entered law school with one three-year class and
graduated with the succeeding three-year class. At least 95 percent of our class were veterans who were primarily interested
in getting a degree as quickly as possible. Since the school op-

erated all year round, many of us attended spring, summer, autumn, and winter terms without taking a break. We were relying on funding from the GI Bill and were older and more mature than traditional students. Since everyone knew that I was an infantry veteran who had earned my place as an equal in a multiracial society, my unique ethnicity as an Asian American was not a barrier at Chicago.

Compared to combat, survival in school was comparatively easy. While keeping up with my studies was difficult, I was not under the stress of having my life at risk. Prejudice from the white university students was almost nonexistent. Even outside the school, bias was minimal since we had overt support from those who knew of us. After what all of us had been through, whenever we perceived prejudice, we now had the confidence to openly confront such racism.

For example, we once discussed the constitutionality of the internment of Japanese from the West Coast in our law school class. The racial implications of the internment were completely ignored in this discussion, and I became very upset. The Supreme Court cases addressing this constitutional issue had been decided in favor of the federal government's use of its war powers over individual civil rights. I could not tolerate this legalistic argument, so I finally spoke up and said, "I'm from Hawai'i, the place where the enemy attacked us, and we were never thrown into camp. You're trying to tell me that the military, headed by a racist general, had a constitutionally sound reason to throw American citizens like my wife temporarily into a horse stable and then an Arkansas concentration camp fenced with barbed wire, when they were actually in California three thousand miles farther away from the enemy than we were in Hawai'i? Factually, your military necessity argument does not make any sense at all. The reason for internment was fear fired by racial prejudice."

Some of my friends in the class calmed me down, assuring me that they realized internment was an unfortunate event with strong racial undertones. However, as a nisei combat veteran I and my generation were in a position to openly challenge the violation of our civil rights. We could now openly state, "Do not ever tell me that you have a right to throw me in a concentration camp because of my racial ancestry." With public acclamation of our achievements from military and civilian leaders, we earned the right to challenge the Supreme Court's decision and those who agreed with it. With unblemished records as citizens of the United States, Japanese Americans did not need to apologize to anybody because of their ancestry.

Making ends meet during those student days was rough. Aya and I got married before I started law school, so we were living off her salary and my GI Bill allowance. We had a little apartment with a communal toilet on the South Side about six blocks from the University of Chicago campus. For entertainment, we enjoyed movies and baseball. When the Chicago Cubs were in town, every Friday was "Ladies' Day," so we would watch the Cubs play at Wrigley Field in the afternoon. Aya only had to pay a quarter for admission while I paid the regular $1.25. We had "red hots," popcorn, and soft drinks at the stadium and enjoyed several hours of baseball at prices we could afford.

Occasionally I would have friends over for dinner. Bishop Fujitani of the Hongwanji in Honolulu was one dinner guest. He was attending the University of Chicago Divinity School at that time, and I invited him over to our little apartment for dinner. I did the cooking during the week since Aya was working in Evanston, using a recipe for pot roast that Aya taught me. I also steamed some vegetables and rice. In those days there were no rice cookers, so I had to cook the rice in a pot. The dinner was a real treat for Bishop Fujitani, who told me that having pot roast simmered and tenderized over an hour in gravy with rice reminded him of home.

As frugal as we were, we could always have used a little more cash to make ends meet. For about three months I did some clerical work in the evening, but I could not take the hectic schedule of working at night and going full-time to law school in the day; I never had enough time for study and sleep. I finally had to quit. Even though I was not driven to get top grades, I wanted to get passing grades and graduate as quickly as possible. I was able to finish four years of law school in three calendar years, attending each quarter of classes all year long without taking a break. When I graduated in March 1949, I was so anxious to return home that I did not even attend the June graduation ceremony.

Before returning, however, my wife and I visited her family on Long Island, New York. My in-laws had lived in California before the war, but were uprooted and forcefully interned. When they eventually left camp, instead of returning to California they moved to Long Island, where they started a very successful nursery business. Their mums often won blue-ribbon awards at the Waldorf Astoria flower show in New York.

After spending a month in Long Island, I was eager to return to the islands. We left Chicago and traveled to Los Angeles on the Southern Pacific Express. There we caught the *Lurline* for Honolulu. Aya got seasick during the five-day sea voyage. Fortunately, however, there were slot machines on the ship and the one-arm bandits occupied her time so she managed to survive the trip.

When we arrived at Honolulu harbor in May 1949, the six-month-long ILWU dock strike had just been called. This union strike, challenging the economic oligarchy of the Big Five, was one of the many major changes taking place in the islands. The union movement was in the islands to stay. As a bystander with other priorities, I was never directly involved in the conflicts of the labor movement. The first thing I needed to do was to pass the bar examination in October. In those months, Aya and I struggled to survive with the very small nest egg we had brought from Chicago. With the strike going on and prices skyrocketing, our funds were quickly being depleted. A dozen eggs were selling for about $1.25 in Hawai'i while back in Chicago they would have cost only 25 cents. At one point we even considered leaving Hawai'i to go back to Chicago, but we decided to stick it out until after the bar examination.

Because I was a veteran, I qualified for a Manoa veterans housing unit, which was located near the present-day Manoa Marketplace. We lived in a single-bedroom apartment in a temporary duplex built for returning veterans. The rent was less than $40 a month, including utilities. My son was born while we lived in the veterans housing. Even though my wife was frugal, we barely made ends meet. One of my brother's friends had an old car that he loaned me for transportation. My family helped, but I still needed to work to earn a little income. Most of my time was devoted to preparing for the bar exam, but fortunately, I was offered a job at a law office for $125 a month to do some legal research. In 1949, $125 went a lot farther than it does today so that job really helped us through some rough times.

When I passed the bar exam in October, I did not have any "political connections" to get a government job. Since I was from an ordinary working-class family who lived thirty miles from downtown Honolulu, none of my relatives or friends knew any influential political power brokers. No one I knew was close to a mover and shaker like Takaichi Miyamoto, who was then closely allied to Mayor Johnny Wilson of Honolulu. With the islands suffering from recession and the economy still reeling from the effects of the big dock strike, finding a job was difficult. There were no positions available in the large *haole* law firms for local-born law school graduates from major mainland universities. These elite firms were importing Caucasian law graduates from major mainland universities.

Fortunately, Ruth Loomis, attorney for the territorial Labor Department, needed a lawyer to assist her in the unemployment compensation division of the department. Although I did not have much hope of getting the job since I was a nobody, Ruth Loomis chose me for the position after personally interviewing all applicants. This was a significant opportunity for me to work and remain in Hawai'i. I stayed at the Labor Department from 1949 until the early months of 1952. The starting salary was $400 a month, a meaningful sum in 1949 for a poor, unemployed married law graduate just starting a family.

Eager to become independent, I left the Labor Department in 1952 and opened my own law office on Alakea Street with Ben Takayesu as my partner. Ben was a 442nd veteran and recent law school graduate from Wisconsin. Other young nisei lawyers in Honolulu were also beginning their careers at the time. Most of us had received our schooling using funds provided by the GI Bill. When we met as a group, we often talked about the economic limitations we faced in Hawai'i. The Big Five represented by the Merchant Street *haole* law firms were still basically in control of the economy and judiciary. While little cracks of opportunity were appearing in business and government, we realized more and more that the only realistic opportunity for our generation to change the socioeconomic environment was through elective politics, where at least we had a chance.

My involvement in the 442nd Veterans Club eventually pulled me into politics. In 1951, I served as the chairman of the "circus committee," an annual fund-raising activity sponsored by the club. The following year, I was elected president of the club, a position that allowed me to establish relationships with leaders of other chapters in the organization. Instead of spending most of my time with the men in Company L, I now had to deal with problems facing all the members of the club. As veterans we knew that if we were to initiate desirable changes in Hawai'i, we needed to become more involved in the overall community and political process. In fact, our issei parents were looking to us to spearhead this change. With the backing of the 442nd, other affiliated veterans organizations, and non-*haole* groups, we were able to form alliances with the local community and government. While we had very limited financial resources, we believed that through the political process we had the voting power to transform the old oligarchic system into a more open society.

In my position as president of the 442nd Veterans Club, I became close to many different veteran and community organizations and helped develop a cohesive group. Since I participated in the University of Chicago's accelerated law degree program, I was able to return to the islands earlier than many of my 442nd peers. Consequently, I was among the first to become involved in the political change that characterized the 1950s.

Of course, we were political novices back in 1950–51. Before the war, the only elections any of us had been involved in were student body elections. As plantation youngsters in rural communities, we never really thought about political parties, elected officials, or voting. Political elections had always been controlled by plantation management. We had a vague idea that Franklin D. Roosevelt was president of the United States and that he had initiated the New Deal to get us out of the Depression. Our primary interest then was personal economic survival and immediate job opportunities, not territorial or national politics.

The postwar era changed that perspective. Our horizons had been expanded by the experience of war and professional education. While we had no previous political experience, many of us were eager to learn. We never even considered that the Republican Party would offer us a political home. Although many older nisei of prewar vintage had joined the Republican Party to align with the ruling elite, that party clearly represented the economic interests and needs of the *haole* oligarchy. The old Republicans never knew quite what to make of us. Although some of them may have considered us a threat to their control, the Party largely ignored us until the political upheaval in 1954, when the Democrats, empowered by nisei veterans, gained control of Hawai'i.

The situation in the Democratic Party was different. A bunch of older nisei mavericks, like Ernest Murai and Mitsuyuki Kido, had been working with Jack Burns, who was then with the Honolulu Police Department. They encouraged many of us in the 442nd club to join them in the Party. Our attraction to the Party was partly ideological, partly a pragmatic recognition that the Party offered us an opportunity to directly participate in the process of organized and traditional party politics. We had a lot of ideas about how to reform Hawai'i, and the Party offered us an official vehicle for change.

The Democratic Party at that time was represented by men like Mayor Johnny Wilson, who was well liked and widely accepted by the public. Another well-known Democrat was Judge William Heen, a former senator, a lawyer, and a political conservative, who got along with the Republican majority. In prewar Hawai'i, the Democratic Party's ethnic base was more part-Hawaiian and Hawaiian. They had joined the Party in opposition to the overthrow of the Hawaiian monarchy by white businessmen represented by the Republican Party. When we first approached the Party and began participating in elections in the precincts, this older leadership felt threatened. The nisei veterans were considered young upstarts bent on rocking the boat. The old-timers resisted, but the change in Party control was inevitable.

Jack Burns especially realized the importance of revitalizing the Democratic Party with young, returning veterans. He drew in people like Dan Aoki, Bill Richardson, Dan Inouye, Sakae Takahashi, Herman Lum, Mike Tokunaga, and, later, myself. Holding informal meetings in the basement of City Hall where Jack was the civil defense director, we learned to understand and use the political process to gain control of the Democratic Party. Convinced that the only real opportunity for meaningful change was through politics, we began in earnest to revitalize and take control of the Democratic Party. And with the strong united base of the 442nd and 100th Battalion veterans, in time we began to control the majority of precincts in the Democratic Party.

In the early days, I did not know Burns personally. But I had heard of him during the war and during my time in law school when he started to recruit veterans. With no prior credentials in politics, I was simply one of many veterans returning home to find work. In the early days of our political effort, the goals of Burns and the nisei veterans were somewhat different. Burns wanted to build a strong Democratic Party with a full slate of candidates to challenge the Republicans in elections. The interest of the veterans, however, was not the same. For us, the Party was not an end in itself, but only a vehicle through which to achieve our hopes and aspirations for a better Hawai'i. While the Party structure could be used to oppose the Republicans in elective politics, we knew that the island-wide support of the 442nd veterans was more important than the Party if we wanted to win elections.

We discussed the possibility of fielding a 442nd veteran candidate for public office for several years. I was chosen to be the first candidate because in 1952 I had become a local public figure through my involvement in the famous "Connally Caravan." Tom Connally, a U.S. senator from Texas, had publicly stated that Hawai'i did not deserve statehood because the majority of the people in the islands were not white. Hal ("Akuhead") Lewis, a popular radio personality, used this racially biased statement to whip up public support for statehood. Akuhead promoted a caravan made up of island veterans and a gold star mother to respond to Connally's racist statement. We wanted to display Hawai'i's World War II record. Hawai'i did deserve statehood. Hawai'i's multicultural people were a showcase for the nation, and the caravan was primed to show that Hawai'i's contribution to the war exceeded that of other states. Since I was president of the 442nd Veterans Club at that time, I was chosen to represent the nisei in this caravan along with three other combat veterans of different ethnic backgrounds. The caravan also included a Texas veteran from the 36th Division, the Texas lost battalion in France that the 442nd rescued. The 442nd was calling in a favor. With extensive local media coverage, plus some national media coverage in Washington, D.C., we successfully confronted the Texas senator for his racist remarks.

Due to this media exposure in 1952, my name was the most recognizable among the 442nd veterans within the community. After assessing our political strength, we thought that a seat on the Honolulu Board of Supervisors was an elective position we could possibly win and I was the natural choice. The Democratic leadership, however, had other ideas. In 1952, the only candidate running for the territorial senate from the Fourth District was an incumbent. With two senatorial seats for that district, there was a vacancy on the ticket. The Party leaders, especially Burns, tried to induce me not to run for the Board of Supervisors, which was filled with candidates, but to file for the vacant senatorial spot. Having a full slate would help the Party. Although I was very reluctant, I agreed to consider it. The whole idea was very quickly dropped, however, when we realized that I was underage and did not qualify as a candidate.

We veterans immediately decided that we would proceed as originally planned with or without the support of Party leadership. In that first election we organized various 442nd veteran groups throughout Oahu. This was to become the real core of our organization. We did not depend on the Democratic Party.

While being a 442nd veteran was critical to my election, I did not want the 442nd Veterans Club, as an organization, to be officially involved in my political campaign. As soon as I declared myself a candidate, I resigned as president of the club so the organization would officially remain nonpolitical. The board wanted me to stay on, but I persuaded them to accept my resignation.

During this period, the Democratic Party was in transition. The old-line Democrats were led by Honolulu City Mayor Johnny Wilson, while another faction was led by Hawai'i's appointed Democratic Governor Stainback. Wilson's faction was based in the city and county government, while Stainback's was in the territorial government, made up of people who had been appointed by the Democratic White House in Washington. Then there was the Burns group, with its core composed of older nisei and other local veterans. The ILWU under Jack Hall had yet another faction, which began to exert its influence in the Party through control of local precincts. The veterans, however, won control of the Party by winning the majority of precinct elections. The nisei veterans reached consensus with other Democratic factions and an acceptable Party platform was drawn up. As a Party, we could support all Democratic candidates seeking office against the Republicans. While infighting within the Party still persisted, we were able to hold these factions together, creating the coalition responsible for the Democratic landslide of 1954.

During our early campaign, we researched the size and demographics of each precinct. We studied the voter profiles, the ethnic makeup of the community, and the various voting patterns. Recognizing that we did not want to waste our time and money trying to reach groups that would probably not vote for us, we spent little time in affluent, predominantly *haole* areas like Manoa or Nuuanu Valleys. The grassroots campaign effort was concentrated in areas where we knew we would have the best chance of getting the votes, working very closely with sympathetic organizations and groups in each precinct. The key to winning the elections, we learned, was to make effective use of our time, to maximize our effort. No candidate could expect to receive every vote; all we needed to win was to have more than 50 percent.

The campaign process was exhausting and time-consuming. As a candidate, I was required to attend four or five political rallies almost every night, running from one to the other and giving basically the same speech over and over again. The formula for political speech-giving in those days was very basic. First, I told the audience my name, explaining that I was a lawyer. I stressed that I wanted to do what was best for the majority of the people. Usually my speeches were very general and vague, lasting only about two minutes. I was basically only trying to sell my name. At coffee hours I would have the chance to sit down with people to talk a little more about the issues of city governance. Electioneering for me was superficial and exhausting, an experience that I never truly enjoyed.

In 1952, the only public media were the daily papers and radio. Television was nonexistent. Candidates used cards or handouts that were distributed to the public by their supporters. Utilizing families, friends, veterans, and supporters, we had enough manpower to conduct a grassroots, house-to-house campaign. With this type of campaigning, we were very successful at reaching the electorate on a one-on-one basis. One of the tactics we first developed was a telephone network, where we asked friends to personally call their friends, who in turn were asked to call their friends for support. Personal cards, preferably handwritten notes, were then sent to everyone asking them for support. This one-on-one contact with friends became a powerful political tool that is still used in Hawai'i's elective politics. Fortunately, sign-holding on the streets was not in vogue in those days.

Campaign funds largely came from family members and friends, who usually contributed $5, $10, or $25. A contribution of $100 was considered a substantial donation. During my campaign, we raised a couple thousand dollars, which was used to print political placards and cards. Staff meals, gas, and other incidental expenses came out of my supporters' own pockets. My brother-in-law used his kitchen at Charlie's Arcade in downtown Honolulu to prepare *bentos* for campaign workers on election day, contributing rice and other foodstuffs. Compared to today's cost of campaigning, my campaign costs were very small. While we knew the exact amount of money collected and spent, there was no way to measure the value of the donations of rice, food, gasoline, and time contributed by friends.

The daily newspaper coverage of my campaign was very limited. In the press I was viewed as the "new kid," who was associated with the "Connally Caravan" and the 442nd. Although I was characterized as a young lawyer who spoke very well, I was an unknown quantity. I was given only an outside chance of being elected. However, we felt our grassroots effort would succeed. In addition to the veterans' active involvement, I was able to receive wide community support and was elected to the Board of Supervisors. In our first attempt at elective politics, we succeeded.

One of the results of the 1952 election was that we had learned to conduct an effective island-wide campaign. Within the Fourth and Fifth Districts of Oahu, we had learned how to mobilize support groups within the electorate. The first taste of victory was indeed sweet. With our newly created political base, the social and political revolution we had long dreamed of seemed within our grasp.

CHAPTER THREE

At the Heart of a Revolution

THE EXHILARATION FOLLOWING our political victory at the polls soon abated as the realities of governing became clear. As a newly elected member of the Board of Supervisors, I quickly realized that I was only one vote out of seven. The many changes we as veterans had envisioned could not occur simply by my saying, "I'm going to do this!" To effectively spearhead change, I needed the skills of a negotiator. I had to sit down with the rest of the supervisors and persuade them to take a certain course of action.

The three Democrats on the board in 1952 were Noble Kauhane, Mitsuyuki Kido, and myself. The four Republicans were Sam Apoliana, Milton Beamer, Nicholas Teves, and Johnny Asing. Although a majority, the Republicans could not organize the board. There were two Republicans who were willing to work with the Democrats. There was one Republican maverick and another Republican who was by then old and more interested in fixing potholes in the roads for his constituents than organizing the board. With the support of the two Republicans open to working with us, the control of the board was largely put in the hands of the Democrats. In those days, the Board of Supervisors worked well with the Democratic mayor Johnny Wilson, who set a conciliatory tone to government at City Hall.

When Neal Blaisdell later became mayor in 1954, I led the board in its stonewalling efforts against him because I was not certain how he would align himself in the Kalihi Tunnel litigation. During the construction of the tunnel, a major structural disaster resulted in the deaths of several construction workers, with the city exposed to millions of dollars in damages. The contractor refused to assume liability for the accident, shifting blame to the city and county. Blaisdell was the newly elected Republican mayor and seemed to have a working relationship with the contractor. Doubtful of his intentions, I used my position with the majority on the board to block many of the mayor's actions and appointments. However, as soon as Blaisdell was able to convince us that he had the interests of the city first, we started working together. Eventually we became good friends. We learned to trust him, and the mayor and the board worked well together during the rest of Blaisdell's tenure.

Indeed, during my years with the board, I learned that an effective political policymaker is someone with a clear goal or objective who is willing to work diligently behind the scenes, building consensus to achieve those ends. In my view, the politician who plays to the media for his or her own political interests at the expense of others is ultimately ineffective with peers. I always tried to work with the majority of the board. I would not make personal political hay by discrediting the others. In controversial cases with political risks, I learned to take the heat and lead in the decision-making. If at all possible, it was more effective to work in the background and let somebody else receive credit in order to build political consensus and exert leadership. Since symbolic titles were also of little interest to me, I gladly exchanged a title for support to govern effectively.

Another limitation on my ability to effect political change was the limited scope and jurisdiction of city and county government. The territorial legislature had the power to enact laws and appropriate funds affecting the entire territory, including the county governments. The Democratic majority's priorities in the 1950s were to push for reform in tax laws and to expand educational opportunities. The democratically controlled legislature after 1954 began to enact critical laws to effectively change policy in the areas of tax reform, education, labor laws, and business. The county government did not have this legislative power. The board dealt mostly with issues such as roads, sewers, and zoning. At each legislative session, the counties went hat in hand to seek help from the legislature. However, there was one advantage. We governed all year, not just during a sixty-day legislative session. Also, the county government affected the lives of the people more directly than the legislature by virtue of its dealing with problems of police, parks, water, roads, sewers, and land development. We were closer to the daily lives of the people within our county, but we did not have the power to pass basic policymaking laws. As a supervisor I took every opportunity I could to sit down with legislators and discuss important legislative matters affecting the county.

During my tenure as supervisor, I also became close to Jack Burns, who at the time was the head of the Office of Civil Defense under Mayor Wilson. Since Burns' office was also in City Hall, I often visited with him in his downstairs room, joining a small group of young activist veterans to discuss Democratic Party strategies and reforms. During those meetings we articulated our hopes and aspirations for greater opportunities for all people, particularly the local "have-nots," and for lessening the power of the "haves" on Merchant Street. Quite frankly, we wanted to break the economic stranglehold of the Big Five in Hawai'i. The old power structure, however, never really understood the changes happening in Hawai'i or that these changes meant an overthrow of their past political power and status until it was too late. Our attention in these planning sessions was also directed to the next Party convention and the platform for the Democratic Party. The Burns group tried to restructure that platform to reflect our concerns about land, tax, and education.

The so-called Bloodless Revolution of 1954 was the fulfillment of our political dreams. The Democratic Party, with its sweeping, reform-minded platform, assumed undisputed control over both houses of the territorial legislature for the first time. With many of the newly elected freshmen legislators being nisei veterans, the liberation of Hawai'i from the past seemed at hand. The Party began to change the laws of Hawai'i.

One of the most important changes we wanted was to tax land based on its highest and best use in order to break open unused but valuable vacant land. We also wanted to level the playing field in government to ensure that the people of Hawai'i would be considered for employment based on their ability rather than race or color. We wanted changes in the labor laws, including an increase in the minimum wage to guarantee livable compensation for working people. Many small business employers, many of whom were nisei, complained that raising the minimum wage would hurt their businesses. We explained to them that everyone had to have at least a subsistence wage level. If all businesses had to deal with the problem on an equal basis, then it would not affect any particular business adversely. Everybody had to pay the same minimum wage. As the legislative process of changing the economic and social structure was taking place, we recognized that some groups that supported us would feel the pain of change. Our goal, however, was to be as fair as possible to everyone.

We saw the potential growth of tourism as an industry, with new and different players. We realized the Big Five were important players in Hawai'i's economy, and we did not want to destroy them. However, we did not want them to continue to dominate and be the only game in town. Tourism would open up all kinds of economic avenues for the future, providing opportunities for the upcoming generation of those outside the existing economic oligarchy.

In that sense, our social and economic goals were not revolutionary. We wanted to accelerate the changes that had begun during the war, not destroy the system. Many *haole* businessmen fled the war zone of Hawai'i and went to the mainland following the Pearl Harbor attack. That exodus created an economic vacuum for local entrepreneurs to fill. They took over the abandoned businesses or bought unused property, and expanded their interests in various businesses such as restaurants, supermarkets, and durable goods dealerships.

Land development and residential subdivisions, construction of commercial and industrial buildings, and home-building were being started and completed by local businessmen. These activities enlarged the economic base of these local entrepreneurs as small businesses evolved into sizable companies, such as Servco-Pacific, Times Supermarket, and Star Supermarket. The Fukunagas of Servco started a small garage in Haleiwa, which grew into a large conglomerate of auto and durable goods dealerships, discount stores, and financial institutions. The Fujieki family started a small family market that grew into the Star Supermarket chain. The Teruyas' small restaurant and market in the 1950s and 1960s eventually became Times Supermarket. Chinn Ho started Capital Investment. K. J. Luke and Clarence Ching created Loyalty Enterprises, while Aloha Airlines began with Ruddy Tongg. As the number of local professionals, lawyers, and doctors grew in postwar Hawai'i, the economic, professional, and political landscape also changed rapidly.

When Sears came to Honolulu, the Big Five (through Liberty House) could no longer control the local department store market. Large mainland businessmen such as Henry Kaiser challenged the old guard with real estate development projects in the islands. Kaiser's enormous economic muscle and independence, derived from sources outside Hawai'i, weakened the once omnipotent Big Five. The introduction of mainland enterprises such as Sears and Kaiser to Hawai'i in the 1950s and 1960s did much to diversify and change the economic climate. These economic changes ran parallel with the political changes that were accelerating with the emergence of the new Democratic Party.

The Democratic Party conventions during the 1950s served as the incubator for these new democratic forces of change. The various Party factions frequently became very contentious during the Party convention. The Heen and Stainback groups walked out during the 1956 convention after the Burns group took over the proceedings. When Stainback was governor of the Territory of Hawai'i, all appointments to the executive and judiciary branches of the government were determined by the White House in Washington, D.C. Local-born, non-white Democrats with no mainland connections had little chance of being appointed. The governor was clearly more concerned about his relationship with Washington than those in the islands. During Stainback's tenure, the common joke was that it was better to be from Tennessee than Hawai'i if you wanted to be appointed to the Hawai'i judiciary—a comment containing more truth than humor. As a result, the local, non-white Democrats felt no allegiance to the governor or the power brokers in Washington. We viewed ourselves as the neglected stepchildren of Washington's national politics.

There was pressure from other factions in the Democratic Party, such as the ILWU, to push their own political agenda. This further complicated intra-Party matters. In 1956, the ILWU attempted to take over the Democratic Party, an effort that resulted in bitter division within the Party. At that year's Democratic convention, there were several precinct battles with supporters of the ILWU. The Burns group and I worked with my 442nd and 100th Battalion friends to take over these precincts from the ILWU faction. Many others were similarly successful in efforts to limit the influence of the ILWU at the precinct level. The old-line Democrats aligned with Mayor Wilson had little real support in the precincts. By the time of the convention, the Burns group had enough votes to control the convention. In fact, I was the one assigned to carry the proxies in my pocket to assure complete control of the convention.

When we finally prevailed in these intra-Party struggles, our group tried to be as accommodating to the losing faction as possible. We talked with the leaders of the ILWU and established a working relationship with Mayor Wilson and his supporters in City Hall. However, we found it difficult to negotiate with the Stainback group, which had a markedly different agenda from ours. By election time, however, we were able to soothe some of the hurt egos and present a united political front against the Republicans.

Jack Burns increasingly became the central figure in coalescing the Democratic Party's common front. In part, his effectiveness was due to his belief that perceptions of ethnic inferiority had to be erased. He repeatedly stressed that whatever our backgrounds or ethnicities, we were as good as anyone else. By his words and actions, he reminded us that this was as much our community as anyone else's. The Japanese, Hawaiians, Chinese, the non-*haole* groups, he emphasized, are as good as the whites. "You need not feel inferior," he would tell us. "You are as good as the next guy. Feel it and believe it. Do not apologize for your ethnic background; it is irrelevant. Only your ability counts."

His understanding and involvement with the multiracial culture of Hawai'i began early in life. He was raised in Kalihi by a mother who worked at the post office, and he attended St. Louis High School with other local people. During the war he became a captain in the police force, and was assigned to internal security to work with military intelligence. Many of the older issei thought that he was responsible for putting their friends and leaders in internment camps during the war. They called him *inu*, or "dog," an informer who betrayed the Japanese. Those of us who worked with him knew otherwise. When the accusation sometimes arose that Burns had helped incarcerate Japanese during the war, we repeatedly explained that he actually helped the Japanese. Conditions would have been much worse without him since he took measures to prevent an escalation of reprisals against the resident Japanese. Burns had worked very closely with the Japanese community's morale committee. Knowing the loyalty of the issei and nisei, he actively opposed the wholesale removal of Japanese from Hawai'i. He supported the interests of the local Japanese whenever he could while working in the sensitive internal affairs of military and civilian intelligence. Burns did much to ameliorate the wartime hysteria against our families and friends. For that reason the 442nd Club made John Burns an honorary member.

Initially, I wondered whether Burns was for real. I suspected that we were being used by him. And, to be quite honest, we considered how we could use him. However, as I got to know him I recognized that he spoke from his heart. What he said he was trying to do was not just rhetoric. He deeply believed in his vision of equality.

My affection for Jack Burns was not only political. I grew to like him personally. We shared the same hopes and aspirations, and I admired his strength of character. My wife and I also became very close to his wife, Bea Burns, who was an extraordinary individual. Even though stricken with polio and confined to a wheelchair, Bea was a pillar of strength. She was also a truly caring person. She did not suffer from self-pity. She had been through adversity and accepted her handicaps. Her needs were minimal, and both Jack and Bea were very frugal. All his friends knew the financial hardships they experienced throughout the 1950s. Jack Burns paid a high price for his belief in us, and we, in turn, responded to him. He had earned our loyalty.

The question of Jack Burns' sincerity became a critical issue when it came to fund-raising for his campaigns. The Burns campaign had limited resources in those days when Republicans controlled the major money spigots. When I called on successful local non-white businessmen to raise money for Burns, I had to convince them that he really wanted to do what he said and that he could win. More and more I became convinced that if the nisei veterans were to achieve our larger goal of a more democratic Hawai'i, we must elect Jack Burns to head the Democratic ticket.

Burns was willing to make the necessary political sacrifices. That drew his supporters closer to the man, his vision, and his values. I remember vividly his 1954 campaign against Joe Farrington as delegate to the U.S. Congress. Burns knew he was not going to win. Yet with the Party needing someone to head the ticket, he agreed to enter the contest even though he was very strapped for cash and was electioneering for a losing cause. During that campaign his family depended on his wife, who ran a small liquor store. He was often seen campaigning with holes in his shoes. When he ran again for delegate in 1956 against Betty Farrington, all of us thought he had a chance. During that campaign I sent my whole political organization to help him, devoting more of my time to his campaign than to my reelection for supervisor. While I won, Jack again suffered defeat.

Through the experiences in the 1950s, deep loyalties and friendships were formed and the Democratic Party became a formidable force in the islands. The Party was not a political machine based on patronage and economic self-interest. Our bonds were based on friendship and a common mission. The same kind of loyalty we felt on the military battlefields we now exhibited on the political battlefields. Again, our loyalty stemmed from the ethnic values we had learned from our Asian culture, especially the Japanese notions of personal obligation, which played a significant part in building and strengthening this network. The personal relationship I formed with Jack Burns was one of mutual respect and devotion, which only deepened over the years. While this political network has been misrepresented by some critics as an all-powerful political machine, it was actually born in the plantation communities, nurtured through our war experiences, and refined with schooling.

Although his 1956 election bid was unsuccessful, Jack knew what I had done to help his campaign. He also knew that I had regarded his election as more important than mine to the people of Hawai'i. We had come very close to victory in this 1956 election. Jack's long search for political success finally ended in 1958, when he was elected delegate to the U.S. House of Representatives. Now he finally had the chance to prove his worth to Hawai'i. Statehood was his first and most important priority.

For those nisei who had served in World War II, making Hawai'i an equal partner among all the other states in the federal government was a crucial goal. To be able to elect our own governor and representatives to Congress was an essential benchmark of first-class citizenship. For an elected governor to appoint the judges within a state judiciary system with the advice and consent of a state senate was the hallmark of being part of a full-fledged democracy. We wanted to be treated equally in funding, like all other states, and not remain a stepchild of the White House and Congress. Statehood quite simply meant controlling our own destiny in the islands.

When he was elected delegate, Jack Burns pushed us to the forefront of the statehood effort. He kept telling us that for statehood, the multiracial population was a plus and not a minus. "Do not be ashamed of who you are. Talk about your war record. You guys deserve it. You have proven that you are Americans. You earned this honor under fire. Flaunt it." He led us in the statehood movement, encouraging us to be up-front, repeating how much we had to offer Hawai'i and the nation, and how much Hawai'i had to offer the nation from a global perspective.

The Big Five were ambivalent about statehood. Territorial status meant control from Washington, D.C., where they had the best contacts with the power brokers of the nation. We learned that they were discreetly discussing how to remain a territory in their cocktail circuit. They wanted to retain political control even if they lost their voting base. With all their connections in Washington, they seemed to have greater influence than we did in the appointment of the governor, as well as the judges, no matter who was president. The affluent white *kamaaina* groups knew that they would have a difficult time electing a governor under statehood. While they could not publicly come out against statehood, it was clear to some of us that they certainly were not pushing the cause as hard as they could.

Many Hawaiians were not sure that statehood would help them. Some wanted the equal status of statehood under the American system. Others were not supportive for a variety of reasons, not the least of which were ill-feelings still left over from the overthrow of the Hawaiian monarchy. In addition, some must have been concerned that the up-and-coming nisei generation would have greater power and control of the islands than they. Many Hawaiians also identified more closely with the white *kamaaina* families than with the non-white political mavericks challenging the status quo of Hawai'i.

Despite the various opposition groups, the statehood movement kept marching on. When Jack Burns was elected in 1958, the first thing he did in Washington was to form a close relationship with the congressional Democratic leadership led by Sam Rayburn, the Speaker of the House, and later, Lyndon Johnson, the Majority Leader in the Senate. Jack understood the congressional power structure and political process in Washington and knew what he had to do to be successful. His biggest concern was the Southern Democratic bloc, which looked upon Hawai'i as being too liberal on civil rights issues. Jack decided that if he could not get the active support of these old, patriarchal Southern senators and representatives, at least he could gain their passive nonresistance. In the case of Senator Russell Long of Louisiana, Jack and a friend from Louisiana were actually able to win him over to active support of Hawai'i's statehood. We later repaid our debt to Lyndon Johnson for his critical support on statehood by standing behind him for the presidency at the 1960 Democratic convention.

Another strategy that Jack Burns pursued was to allow Alaska to become a state before Hawai'i. He knew that this strategy was politically risky in Hawai'i, but he was convinced that if a Republican-dominated Alaska came into the Union before Hawai'i, the GOP would be mollified about a Democratically controlled Hawai'i becoming a state. In effect, Alaska and Hawai'i would check and balance each other along party lines during votes on crucial national issues. The contiguity and population issues raised in opposition to Hawaiian statehood would also dissipate with Alaskan statehood. Strategically, it made political sense. Burns helped push Alaska to statehood first, with a commitment from the Alaskan delegation that they, in turn, would support Hawai'i.

During all these negotiations, Jack kept nurturing his relationship with the two congressional leaders from Texas, Sam Rayburn and Lyndon Johnson. Both Texans liked Jack Burns personally. Both men certainly must have known that the 442nd rescued the lost battalion since the State of Texas, through a proclamation signed by Governor John Connally, declared all members of the 442nd Regiment "honorary Texans." While left unsaid publicly, such a strong wartime affiliation must have somehow influenced them to support statehood for Hawai'i. In 1959, Alaska became the forty-ninth state and Hawai'i followed as the fiftieth state of the Union. Jack Burns' strategy had worked. He deserved a lot of credit for Hawai'i's final achievement of statehood.

With Hawai'i now the fiftieth state, Jack Burns was the natural choice as the Democratic gubernatorial candidate. However, Burns returned to Hawai'i late in the campaign season. Due to overconfidence and various miscalculations and mistakes, he lost the governor's race in 1960 to Republican Bill Quinn, who had been the last appointed territorial governor and therefore an incumbent. Two years later, more focused and mobilized, Burns and his Lieutenant Governor William Richardson won the 1962 gubernatorial election, defeating Governor Quinn.

I remember the first inauguration of John A. Burns as governor, a landmark of major change in Hawai'i. My wife and I were invited to sit in the special section of the governor-elect. Without our knowing, Clarence Maki, a member of the staff of Honolulu Mayor Neal S. Blaisdell, took our photograph. In a personal letter to me, Mayor Blaisdell called the photograph "a masterpiece in capturing the pride and pleasure our Governor's right-hand man felt in watching Jack Burns inaugurated." The letter continued:

> The thoughtfulness and intensity of Ayako's expression indicate that the new administration has the dedicated backing of all who worked so hard to make the Democratic mandate such an emphatic choice of the people. From my long experience working with you, Matsy, I know that Governor Burns is most fortunate that you and your wife are in the "front row," a reassuring sight for the man looking out from a post of high responsibility.
>
> I hope this picture will help you retain the pleasure of the occasion during the course of our new administration.

This considerate letter and the sentiment expressed illustrate the understanding by both of us of the beginning of a permanent change in Hawai'i.

In 1966, Bill Richardson accepted the position of Chief Justice of the Hawai'i Supreme Court, leaving a vacancy in the lieutenant governor's office. Jack Burns wanted Kenneth Brown as his running mate, but Tom Gill had already declared his candidacy for that post. Some of us were called to a meeting where Burns informed us that he preferred Kenny Brown as his running mate. Kenny Brown, an architect with an impressive Hawaiian lineage, had outstanding credentials. The governor liked him and felt that if anybody could run the state government after he retired, it was the fiscally conservative Kenny Brown, who shared many of the same hopes and aspirations for Hawai'i. He would also symbolize the return of someone of Hawaiian ancestry to the head of government in Hawai'i.

However, to many Democrats Brown was a newcomer and unacceptable since he came from an old-line Republican family. His uncle, Francis Brown, had been a popular Republican state senator. We told the governor that we believed it would not work, but Jack was committed to his choice. He wanted Brown, and if we helped, he believed the nomination had a chance. A qualified part-Hawaiian, he argued, should be running in the race for one of the top slots in the state. While we understood where he was coming from, a realistic political appraisal indicated that Brown would not be electable against someone like Gill. Still, we pledged our support to him because this was what he wanted. When Brown lost in the primary to Gill, Burns blamed himself for Brown's loss. In the gubernatorial election that year, Burns seemed to have lost the desire to campaign. In fact, his campaign was so lackluster with Gill as his running mate that he nearly lost the governor's race in the general election.

During those years I tried to keep a low public profile. Titles had little meaning to me, especially if they were merely symbolic positions. I deliberately stayed away from the glare of the media. My contribution was working in the background and calling on people privately for help. I also knew that I had a certain amount of leverage within the community as a councilman to rally political support for Burns. My personal closeness to Jack Burns was well known and helped me to garner support for his campaigns. The fact that I had also become closely affiliated through my law practice with many businessmen in financial circles helped. To work privately in the background, away from the media, was the best way I got support.

As a governor, Jack Burns always did what he thought was right. I never interfered. He had good instincts and judgment as well as a strong sense of character and heart. I never said anything unless asked. Despite the criticism that comes with the job, Jack Burns always did the best he could, showing his concern and compassion for people, especially the weak and poor. He had an extraordinary understanding of the islands' political and social systems, and did not allow his ego to interfere with a vision of a new Hawai'i. History, I believe, will place him as one of the great governors of Hawai'i.

During my political career, I learned that dealing in politics was quite different from dealing in business. In business, either the deal is on or it is off. Both sides of the negotiations have to feel that they are benefiting from the deal. Overreaching is the beginning of a fractured business relationship. Both parties have to be prepared to give and take, knowing the options available to them and the risks they are taking. The deal that is finally settled upon should be fair and reasonable to both parties, with an eye to creating a lasting relationship.

In politics, however, the ultimate bottom line is power, based on how many votes each party carries. If a party is in the minority, it can only sit on the sidelines and challenge and harass the majority. Because votes shift, politics can be volatile and unpredictable, with egos often getting in the way. Politics, as is often said, therefore makes strange bedfellows.

During the 1950s and 1960s, some very powerful personalities emerged in the political arena in addition to Governor Burns. Hiram Fong was one of these leaders. He had served as

Speaker of the House in the state legislature and later as a U.S. senator. Fong was not a "Republican" in the traditional, white Merchant Street mold. Elected because he was a "local," his political base was largely from the populace. He developed an independent, local image that was unencumbered by the albatross of white Merchant Street affiliation. As a lawyer and businessman with a non-white political base, Fong, a Republican, was not so different from a moderate Democrat.

Tom Gill, the aggressive head of the liberal wing of the Democratic Party, was different. The Burns faction was moderate, independent, and relatively conservative on fiscal policies. While they were sympathetic to labor, they were also concerned about business, especially small business. Labor would always be given an audience, but the Burns faction was not going to be controlled by them. Tom Gill, however, was more labor-oriented. Born and raised in Hawai'i, Gill was not a member of a chosen *kamaaina* family. Instead of attending the exclusive Punahou School with most other *haole* elite, he attended Roosevelt High School, a public school. When he came back to Hawai'i from law school, Gill represented the Art Rutledge–led labor unions, and he became the leader and spokesman of the party's labor-oriented faction. When Gill refused our overtures to reach an accommodation within the broad structure of the Party, we parted into competing and often conflicting factions with a different agenda and priorities.

There was never any real accommodation after that. The division flared up at the county and state conventions, where there was a struggle for internal Party control that evolved into organizational infighting in the legislature. Unaligned legislators blurred the lines between these factions with powerful egos. Political muscle moved individuals one way or another until a majority was put together. Leadership and control were at stake in these struggles, which sometimes left deep, bitter, long-lasting scars.

George Ariyoshi was another leader who impacted the political scene during this period. He had started his career in the House and then went on to the state senate. In 1970, when Tom Gill, then lieutenant governor, decided to challenge Jack Burns for the governorship, the lieutenant governor's office became vacant. Ariyoshi declared for the office, aligning himself with Burns, while Nelson Doi, Ariyoshi's primary opponent, aligned himself with Gill. During this landmark election in Hawai'i politics, the Burns campaign put together a brilliant film entitled *To Catch a Wave,* a provocative production that depicted the changes that had helped create opportunities for all people throughout the eight years of Burns' administration. Jack Burns won his final election with George Ariyoshi as his lieutenant governor. When Burns became seriously ill with cancer during his final term, Ariyoshi became acting governor. In the next election, Ariyoshi was successfully elected to that office, becoming the titular head of the Democratic Party.

There were other Democratic leaders who also represented the emergence of the Party in Hawai'i. Sparky Matsunaga successfully went from the state House to the U.S. House of Representatives. After Hiram Fong retired from the U.S. Senate, Sparky beat Patsy Mink, who had been in the House of Representatives, in the 1982 senatorial election. Senator Matsunaga stayed in that post until he passed away in 1992. He was very influential in the Senate and established the Matsunaga Institute for Peace. Sparky was especially helpful to me as trustee of the Bishop Estate on tax matters. He was a senior member of the Senate Finance Committee and, equally important, a member of the Congressional Conference Committee on Taxation, which determines the final version of all tax legislation passed by Congress. We lost an influential friend and counsel in Washington when Sparky passed away.

Dan Inouye has always been in a class by himself. Extremely charismatic, with a wonderful, sonorous speaking voice, Dan was the role model of political success for the returning veterans of the 442nd. With Sparky, who was from the 100th battalion, he personified the culmination of political success in the United States of World War II nisei veterans. They proved beyond a shadow of a doubt that what Burns believed was true—that we could be as good as anyone if we believed it and worked diligently to show what we were capable of doing. Dan was also personally close to Burns and, although he helped Burns as much as he could during elections, he could not transfer his own popularity at the polls to Burns.

The successes Dan and other nisei accomplished in the political arena, others were trying to attain in business and financial circles. Although involved in electoral politics in the City and County of Honolulu, I had no ambition to seek higher political office. I continued to run for the same position because I could not quit while I was electable. That I survived for sixteen years still amazes me. While I enjoyed the work of governing on the city and county level, I never liked elective politics. Asking for votes and taking demeaning insults were distasteful to me. I hated asking for campaign funds and disliked the whole time-consuming political process of electioneering and vote-getting. I also disliked the media attention. Vote-getting appeared to me to be a popularity contest; perception seemed more important than knowledge in effectively governing a city and county government.

There were also financial considerations. Pay for an elective official was not attractive. My private law practice, business interests, and investment banking generated far greater income. To lose an election, I thought, could be a blessing. I could return to my law practice and business, which were more to my liking. Not only would I be making more money; my family and I could once again enjoy our privacy. The glass house of politics in which we had lived was not appealing. Occasionally I considered quitting, but I could not retire from office as long as my friends who supported me wanted me to run.

I was finally defeated for reelection in the 1968 campaign. One of my friends observed that the reason I lost was because I would say "no" to constituents' wishes and they would be "mad as hell" at me. Others could say "no" and their constituents would not be personally mad at them. Since I was not afraid of losing an election, when circumstances demanded a strong position, I took political risks if I thought doing so was right. Sometimes courage calls for taking unpopular positions.

Once as chairman of the Finance Committee, I took an unpopular, controversial position when I refused to set aside money for the police chief to attend a national police convention. My reasoning was quite simple. Since we had denied requests of other city department heads to attend national conventions because of budget constraints, we could not approve the Police Department's request. Although the media went after me, I did not believe that the police chief should be given preferential treatment. We had to be consistent. The press never let the voters forget this incident. I was castigated by the media during the next election. Although others on the council had agreed with me, I was the point man who received all the heat. At least my conscience was clear and I believed I was right in not making an exception.

I readily accepted my defeat in 1968. My time had come, I said to myself, and I was willing to accept the voters' decision. My family and I were relieved that my political career was over for good. I was forced to retire by the electorate. On election night, when it became apparent that I had lost, Jack Burns called me to express his deep regrets. "Jack, please don't worry," I said to him. "I'm glad it's over. I'm not going to lose any sleep over this. I have no regrets. I'm going to bed!" Although elective politics was over for me, a new chapter in my life was beginning, which would allow me to devote more time to developing my law practice and business interests.

CHAPTER FOUR

The Financial Revolution

BESIDES THE POLITICAL revolution that was transforming Hawai'i, there were also exciting economic changes. Returning veterans were educated, highly skilled professionals seeking greater economic participation within the community. They were teaming up with budding entrepreneurs and older-generation risk-takers in niches of small business activity. The big corporations on Merchant Street never fully comprehended this social uprising, but simply struggled to keep out the competition and maintain the status quo. Those of us who were part of this economic expansion did not set out with specific goals—we sought only the opportunities available to achieve financial growth and security. Ultimately, our efforts helped open doors for all to climb the economic ladder.

My own financial goals have always been relatively simple. As a high school student in a plantation town before the war, I realized society had placed limits on my life. The only real opportunity I had for upward mobility was to fulfill my mother's dream of becoming a *sensei*. Teaching was an achievable career of high repute, offering steady income and a gigantic step up from the plantation. I could not hope to be rich, but only to achieve some financial security within a meaningful profession. As time went on, however, my goal of becoming a teacher was replaced by the desire to go to law school, preferably a good one. The GI Bill of Rights and my wife's support helped make that aspiration a reality, and I graduated from the University of Chicago Law School. In October 1949, I obtained my license to practice law in Hawai'i. My first real job at the

Department of Labor of the Territory of Hawai'i paid $400 a month, which at that time was more than I had ever earned.

When I left the Labor Department in 1952 to enter private practice with my friend, Ben Takayesu, I no longer had a monthly paycheck. My income was based on the fees I earned from my practice after paying all the expenses. This type of independent career entailed risks and was based on my ability to survive as a lawyer. In my practice, I assisted clients in the structuring of financial deals. This legal work also offered me the opportunity to participate in business activities that supplemented the income from my law practice. When I was elected to the Honolulu Board of Supervisors, I received an additional $200 per month for this part-time position, but private practice remained my primary source of income.

By the time I was thirty years old, I was earning enough from my law practice to pay expenses and provide for my family. In order to build an economic foundation, however, I needed not only to save money, but to establish credit and thereby effectively increase my monetary base in order to invest in financial opportunities as they might arise. In those days a person with limited capital had more opportunities to become a successful entrepreneur than today. For example, a small contractor could commit to buying four or five house lots in a twenty-lot development project with a relatively small downpayment. (The developer, in turn, would then use these sales contracts to collateralize his own loan from a lender.) The contractor could build houses on the four or five lots with building materials and financing provided by the building supply houses. When the houses were sold to the ultimate home buyers, the contractor would pay the developer the balance owed for the lots and pay the building supply houses for the materials. With luck, a nice profit could be made. If the first venture was successful, the contractor could repeat the process of building and selling homes.

The growth of these small contracting businesses throughout the 1950s was an important financial opportunity for those outside the *haole* oligarchy. The Big Five were not involved in home-building ventures on such a small scale. In those days, a contractor, particularly of local origin, could not easily borrow directly from Bank of Hawai'i or Bishop Bank (now First Hawaiian Bank), the two major banks that basically controlled the money supply of the Hawaiian economy. Business loans were hard to come by for anyone who was not part of the *kamaaina haole* establishment. Other sources of capital and financing needed to be developed. In earlier days, the issei used a mutual savings system called *tanamoshi* to accumulate enough funds to start a business. Small as it was, the *tanamoshi* served as a resource to finance business activities. However, conventional banking services were generally unavailable to the Japanese in Hawai'i, who were on the outside looking in, having neither the financial power nor the credit to challenge the establishment. Consequently, these contractors had to go to the building supply houses for their financial support, at a higher cost than conventional bank financing. By financing the contractors, the supply companies ran the show, selling the lumber, underwriting construction costs, and then getting paid back first after houses were sold. The balance, if any, went to these contractors.

The need for local banking institutions that would extend financial assistance to nisei entrepreneurs was finally met by Central Pacific Bank (CPB) and (later) the City Bank of Honolulu. Central Pacific Bank was established in the 1950s by World War II veterans like Sakae Takahashi and Dan Inouye, who were encouraged and supported by older nisei like Mitsuyuki Kido. CPB had an impressive record of growth and influence within the Americans of Japanese ancestry (AJA) community, making a major change within the financial structure of Hawai'i. City Bank, under the leadership of nisei like James Morita, further accelerated these changes in banking and business circles. Both of these early nisei-based banks had meaningful financial and administrative support from major Japanese banking institutions. Over the decades, both developed into strong and viable financial entities, reaching a broad-based, multiethnic community. Their contribution to the economy in providing credit to local businesses was undeniably great in the postwar period.

One of the leading financiers who contributed to the post-war economic evolution of Hawai'i was Chinn Ho, a true mover and shaker who helped break the economic strangle-hold of the oligarchy on the business community. A successful stockbroker involved in investment banking, Chinn organized the Capital Investment Company with capital from a large number of local people who sought investment opportunities under his leadership. His board of directors consisted of a broad spectrum of the local population—doctors of Portuguese and Chinese ancestry, a dentist of Japanese ancestry, and a real estate executive of part-Hawaiian ancestry. The company provided local people with an opportunity to invest in island real estate and financial assets. Chinn always appeared cool and relaxed. He was an early riser, who thought about and structured the parameters of an investment during these early hours when he was undisturbed. He would do this with the seasoned instincts of a risk-taker honed by experience and preparation.

Acquisition of the former Waianae Sugar Plantation was his first big deal. Knowing the burning desire of the independent farmers to own their land in fee, he divided the agricultural lands of the former plantation into small-acreage lots for quick sale at a reasonable price. These sales helped him finance the purchase of vast plantation holdings. Just as the returning veterans were contributing significantly to the change in politics, Chinn was changing, transforming, and opening traditional banking and business relationships in Hawai'i.

A project that illustrates Chinn's know-how and skill in structuring a real estate investment was the Lewers Street apartments, a project with which I became involved in 1953 as a lawyer representing his firm. The project involved the construction of a Federal Housing Administration (FHA)–financed high-rise apartment on leasehold lands located on Lewers Street in Waikiki. The zoning was already in place. An elderly couple who owned the land did not want to sell it, so structuring a leasehold that met the requirements of the FHA was the only viable alternative. Sensing the desire of the couple for immediate up-front funds, Chinn structured a deal in which they were paid a substantial rent in advance to meet their present cash need. They would then receive an annual income stream over the term of the lease, which met FHA lease requirements while still retaining the fee interest. Appraisers put a substantial value on the long, below-market leasehold, and that valued together with the value of the projected improvements that would be placed on the property were used to calculate the loan on this project. The loan, in fact, turned out to exceed the costs of construction, but was a perfectly appropriate loan in keeping with FHA policy at that time. I was asked to close the documentation with the FHA for the loan. Timing was critical since the FHA was in the process of changing its regulations and our ability to procure this loan would expire. The new regulations mandated that a loan could be no more than a fixed percentage of the construction cost. Fortunately, we were able to meet the deadline.

This was the start of my learning how to structure a deal. I was not only involved in the formal documentation of the project; I participated in the "number-crunching," weighing and evaluating the risks involved as well as the tax implications. The Lewers Street project broadened my experience and gave me an actual overview of how a deal is made from start to finish.

This was the first time I was involved in this type of financing—and I found it exciting. In the world of finance, I saw the power of money and credit move a project and learned how important it is to structure an investment to use credit effectively. Using credit means leveraging with the lender's money at a cost and convincing the lender that a project can be done and will safely amortize its loan. If one has enough money, the process is simple. Yet building a successful business venture requires skill to minimize and spread the risk, and knowledge of how to use conventional lenders to finance the investment. There are many ways to successfully structure a project, including incremental financing, where one must show increasing value and cash flow to fund the loan. There is no single method of financing a project, and all methods involve some risk. Number-crunching the available options also needs to be done since only through preparation can one determine the risks involved. This is absolutely necessary to acquire lender financing. The world of finance can be harsh and unforgiving. If you are wrong, you can be wiped out.

My experience in assessing the viability of an investment gave me know-how beyond mere legal advice that I could share with my clients. I remember time and again someone would come to seek legal advice on a commercial matter, and I would start by asking a series of questions: "Have you run the numbers? Have you considered the tax implications? Do you have the appropriate business structure to proceed as planned?" I was acting more like a financial consultant than a lawyer, explaining that the legal documentation should reflect the business and financial considerations of their problem. Thus, I was beginning to earn a solid reputation as a "business" lawyer.

This legal and business skill especially helped contractor clients, who would come to me with proposed real estate developments. We first ran the hypothetical numbers, projected a reasonable cost for the raw land, projected the cost of financing the infrastructure (through a building supply house), and then determined the amount of equity needed and the probable rate of return. We ran the break-even point and worst-case scenario to set the downside of the contemplated investment. Clients often took me with them to meet the seller, the investors, and the building supply lenders, asking me to explain and describe the project. To show my confidence in the deal, I also participated in the financing with my own money. The process was always interesting and stimulating, and mostly profitable.

While this was going on, I continued to work with Chinn. He was a charismatic personality and from him I learned the value of hospitality as a means of broadening business connections. His reputation for entertainment was legendary. His business executive friends from the mainland always looked forward to a gourmet Chinese dinner with Chinn and his wife, Betty, who was a great hostess. Their casual and informal hospitality played a significant part in developing and enhancing his business relationships. I had dinner with him often—and only rarely did I see local white *kamaaina* executives at these dinners. In those years, when the Pacific Club was still out-of-bounds for Asian Americans, Chinn's relationship with *haole* businessmen in the islands was not close.

Then came the development of the Ilikai high-rise cooperative apartment. Two developers from the mainland got an option to buy the land from the Dillingham group at a price that was considered very high at that time. In the early 1960s, Waikiki was considered to be on the Diamond Head side of Fort DeRussy. The Ilikai site was on the *ewa* side of DeRussy—thus outside "Waikiki" and still basically undeveloped. The developers were looking for financial support. Chinn reviewed their development plan for a thirty-story high-rise building on that site and negotiated to buy their option.

Recognizing that financing was the key to the completion of the Ilikai project, Chinn also knew that such financing was not available in Hawai'i. Not only would the loan amount stretch the limits of major island banks, but Merchant Street would not look favorably on a local businessman without strong financial resources, especially one with a reputation for taking risks. Sam Silverman—a highly skilled New York mortgage banker—was therefore asked to procure a loan for this project. Sam knew Ed Palmer, the senior officer of First City National Bank of New York (FCNB—now Citicorp), who was responsible for the western region of the United States, including Hawai'i. Sam was able to secure a construction loan from FCNB, which at that time was the largest money market bank in New York. Equitable Life Insurance Company, which had done some major loans in Hawai'i, then committed to a permanent take-out loan.

With these loan commitments in place, it was easy to negotiate a correspondent bank relationship with the Bank of Hawai'i to service these loans. We employed a major mainland architectural firm and entered into a construction contract with Hawaiian Dredging Company, a subsidiary of Dillingham, on a cost plus fixed fee basis, with a maximum cap on the construction amount. As construction started, we found that marketing the apartments as a co-op was going to prove difficult. Condominium ownership was still a new concept. A state statute had been passed patterned after a model FHA condominium statute in which individuals could own their unit along with the common areas for all units. Under this arrangement, each unit could be mortgaged separately. Equitable was willing to provide the mortgage for the individual buyers of these units if we were able to present satisfactory legal documentation preserving the mortgagee's interest.

The most difficult barrier to overcome was fire insurance coverage for the condominiums. In order to procure adequate financing we needed to obtain insurance coverage that would be based on the replacement value of the improvements. Insurance companies resisted this change, wanting to use the depreciated value of the improvements rather than the replacement value. Replacement value recovery, the rationale went, encouraged arson. Finally, a major carrier, Hartford Insurance Company, parent of our local Pacific Insurance Company, agreed to write the kind of policy we needed. With this matter finally resolved, Equitable's take-out financing was firm.

I will never forget the day when the finishing touches for the condominium documentation were worked out with Howard Thomas, general counsel of Equitable. A group of us met in his room at the Royal Hawaiian Hotel. As we were completing the final details, the announcement of the assassination of John F. Kennedy reached us. The date was November 22, 1963. The day the first major lending institution committed funds to finance a condominium project in Hawai'i was a date I would never forget.

As part of Equitable's take-out financing, the company had agreed to finance individual units. With that commitment in place, marketing of the units picked up. However, Chinn Ho then decided to change course. Jets were now flying to Hawai'i, and the hotel industry was beginning to boom. Ed Carlson, president of Western International Hotel, a Seattle-based national hotel chain, had expressed a real interest in the Ilikai. A local hotel management group was put in place and the Ilikai's building plans were changed to accommodate a hotel. Amenities such as a lobby, restaurants, and shops had to be provided. In addition, Chinn wanted an outside glass elevator that would go up to a new restaurant, the "Top of the I." Once the decision was made to include hotel facilities within the Ilikai, the top four floors just below the penthouse level had to be reserved for hotel rooms, along with other amenities, and certain sales within the building had to be suspended. This changed the nature of the financing, which was broken into two distinct parts, the condominium and the hotel.

To cover these changes, Sam Silverman came up with some very creative financing. First, he restructured the loan with Equitable to obtain funds needed to cover some of the changeovers. Then he came up with the idea of using the good credit rating of a third party to secure a short-term loan for the Ilikai from the bank. I was with Sam when he structured this financing. He obtained a guarantee from a major university and paid the university a fee. He then used the good credit rating of the university to borrow funds at a rate lower than he could otherwise obtain. The funds from this short-term loan were used to make the needed changes to the Ilikai, and these changes naturally added value to the structure. This added value, in turn, allowed us to obtain more long-term financing from which we repaid the short-term loan. Additionally, Western International Hotel provided operating funds to cover the shortfalls in the hotel conversion pursuant to the partnership agreement with them. Just being with Sam as he structured deals was a lesson in creative financing—a learning experience that would prove to be invaluable to me.

As the Ilikai development was proceeding, I was approached by a group having trouble with the development of a leasehold interest in Waipahu. They were looking for either a partner or someone to take over their leasehold interest. I reviewed the real estate commitment of the group and the problems they were having in developing the acreage. I wanted only a portion of the land to develop a Tropicana Townhouse, but the fee owners wanted me to take over the entire acreage or they would not consent to the assignment of the lease to me. I asked for a short period to consider the possibility of taking over the entire acreage, exploring ways I could spin it off quickly to minimize the risk. A portion could be used for the townhouse development. GEM, a discount store, had expressed interest in expanding their operation to Waipahu. Royal Amusement was interested in locating a drive-in theater at one end, and it was easy to find a service station interested in using a portion. With time for development, I was fairly confident I could take over the entire acreage, spin off the parcels to other interested parties, and complete the development of the project.

At that time I had already created MAGBA, Inc., my family corporation. ("MAGBA" is a combination of the first letters of the names of myself, my wife, and each of our three children.) I had MAGBA acquire the development rights and worked out a deferred payment plan for the troubled developer. I subdivided the parcel into relatively large lots and obtained a construction loan for development of the infrastructure from the bank. The loan was secured by my personal assets and guarantees. Since MAGBA could not have borrowed such funds based on its own financial statement, my personal commitment was necessary until the bank loan was fully paid.

Developing the land was a relatively easy process. Each lot became a separate leasehold and was allocated a share of the infrastructure cost. MAGBA assigned the leases for the townhouse parcel, GEM, and the drive-in theater for a negotiated premium; it retained a parcel for a small commercial unit and subleased the remaining parcels to various lessees. When the process was completed, the bank loan was paid with funds obtained as reimbursement from each parcel's share of the infrastructure cost and the premiums received for the assignment of leases. After the bank was paid, remaining funds were used to enhance the capital structure of the company. Cash flow to MAGBA continued from the sandwiched portion of the subleases and rental income from the small commercial building on the retained lot. The cash flow from this project provided the funds for the future growth of my family corporation.

While this development of my family corporation was going on, I still maintained my law practice. Chinn suggested to Harry Weinberg that he see me regarding specific problems he was having with the Public Utilities Commission. I told Harry I would not appear before any state agency, but if he needed advice I might be able to help. Though gruff and tough in business negotiations, I learned that beneath his demeanor, Harry had a sincere desire to help the poor and needy. One incident especially struck me as an excellent example of what made Harry "tick."

My wife was asked to chair fund-raising for the Kalani High School marching band so they could go to the Rose Bowl in Pasadena, California. We all sold tickets for *huli huli* chicken, and I was expected by the group to help my wife raise money. I spoke to Harry about helping one of the students whose father was employed in his firm. He said that the employee could afford to pay the expenses to send his daughter on his own. However, he said, if there were any students whose parents could not afford the expense, he would help. I checked, and there were at least six who could not afford to go on the trip without financial assistance. I called Harry and told him about these six students, and, without hesitating, he wrote a check. This compassion for the poor and needy is clearly shown in his will. He would give willingly to Palama Settlement or the homeless, but would turn down funding requests from the Honolulu Symphony. His legacy is kept alive through the Weinberg Foundation, which provides shelter and help for the poor and needy in the islands.

One time Harry called to ask what I thought about twenty acres of land owned by Amfac as an investment. The leasehold on the twenty acres had expired and had been held by a political figure who operated a junkyard on the property. This lessee continued to hold over on the property. Amfac wanted to sell the underlying fee to Harry if he was interested. The land was reasonably priced, but it was unusable as long as the lessee squatted on the lot. Harry asked whether I wanted a piece of the deal if payment for the land was not to begin until Amfac got the lessee out. Since the price and terms of the transaction sounded good, I agreed to take a one-fourth interest for my family corporation. We had a free ride for about two and a half years because Amfac could not get the lessee off the property. When they finally did, we began developing the property.

Development of the land was easy since Harry Weinberg's credit was so good. One day Harry asked whether I would agree to obtaining a loan from the bank at prime to build warehouses on the land. I agreed because I knew full well that it was his corporation's credit, not mine, which got us the loan at prime. We had no difficulty financing the costs of improvements as long as his corporate signature was on the loan, with my corporation only going along for the ride. MAGBA paid its share for the price of land, but all the improvements were financed with bank loans. For about five years all the cash flow went to service debt. Just before he passed away, Harry asked me to agree to pay off the balance of the bank debt. I knew that he wanted to assign his interest to his foundation, and the property had to be debt-free to qualify as a charitable gift generating tax-exempt rental income. He offered to lend my corporation funds to pay off our share of the debt if we needed it. I assured him that this was not necessary, and we paid our share of the outstanding debt to comply with his request. Today this property is debt-free, generating substantial cash flow to both of our entities. If I were to characterize a good investment, this one is by far the best among all the investments the corporation made.

As I look back on my various experiences with financing and investments, I realize that I have made mistakes. For example, for a period of time my standard method of renegotiating loans was based on seeking a fixed rate instead of an adjustable one. This later came back to haunt me. In thirty years, interest rates can change dramatically. What was an above-market rate of return can become a loser. Error in evaluation of a market can also happen. This happened with the Makaha Valley resort. We believed the concept of a Makaha resort, with neighbor island-like experience just an hour away from urban Honolulu, made good sense. Makaha was a beautiful setting, with a golf course, a lush valley, and a quiet and relaxed retreat away from the hustle and bustle of the city.

How wrong we were—the Makaha resort never worked out as we had anticipated.

There is one common thread in all these business and economic activities. Financing is crucial in working the deal, setting the structure and the tone of the investment. Creating a sound financial structure is the crux of a successful investment, and should be cast in such a way to cut losses if the investment turns sour. Financing, I learned, also goes hand in hand with risk-taking.

While I was becoming involved with high-level investment and financing, I also continued to be involved with Democratic Party politics. When Jack Burns was elected in 1962, some unexpected outside analysis about the future of Hawai'i impacted both the economic and political arenas in which I participated. The *Wall Street Journal* ran a front-page article that described Burns as a radical, labor-controlled left-winger and predicted wrenching anti-business changes in Hawai'i. At the time, Chinn and I were scheduled to go to New York City to consummate a loan commitment from Chase Manhattan arranged by Sam Silverman. Both of us were concerned about the *Wall Street* article, which was slanted and basically untrue. We knew the impact this article could have on the credit of the state since the Wall Street investment banking community played such an important part in marketing state bonds. Moreover, the Mauna Kea Beach Hotel was on the drawing board of the Rockefeller group, and we learned that they were deeply concerned about the impact the new governor and his administration might have on their development plans. Coincidentally, the chief executive officer of Chase Manhattan Bank was a Rockefeller and we were meeting senior executives of Chase to work out the loan commitment.

We used this opportunity to send assurances to the Rockefeller group that Governor Burns was not a radical. He looked with favor on the Mauna Kea project. Chinn told the Chase Manhattan executives that I was personally close to the governor-elect. We assured them that the new governor was a fiscal conservative, perhaps more so than the outgoing Republican governor. I also offered to help arrange a meeting of the Rockefeller group's Mauna Kea division and the new governor. We hoped that we had allayed some of the fears and doubts created by the *Journal* article.

The governor understood the importance of nurturing a good relationship with major investment banking institutions in New York. He asked whether a private meeting could be arranged with certain Wall Street decision-makers on his next visit to New York. If he could meet them to share his views and aspirations for Hawai'i, he could assure them that he was no wild-eyed radical. The governor also wanted them to know that he would not institute governmental policies that would jeopardize the creditworthiness of the state. He knew how important it was to create a favorable economic climate in Hawai'i if the state was to continue to have a good credit rating for its bonds.

By this time, I knew Ed Palmer, a senior executive of the First National Bank of New York. I informed him of the governor's interest in meeting privately with senior decision-makers of major lending institutions in New York. Could such a meeting be arranged? He assured me that it could and asked that I call him to set up a meeting when the governor was in New York.

About a month later, Burns was scheduled to attend a governors' conference in Florida. Dan Aoki called me in Honolulu, asking me to arrange a meeting within a few days. I said I would try and called Ed Palmer. With such short notice, Ed said, he was not sure how many executives could come, but he would arrange a meeting at the bank. Working out the details directly with Dan, a private meeting was set up for the governor. Later reports indicated the meeting went as expected. The governor was able to convince those decision-makers present that he would lead a fiscally responsible state administration.

Whenever Ed Palmer was in town during Burns' term as governor, we always had an early private breakfast together if the governor was available. In this informal atmosphere, views were expressed and information exchanged about what was happening in the national and international economy in general and Hawai'i's economy in particular. There was no special agenda for these meetings, which became more and more a meeting of friends—a governor, a senior executive of a major money market bank in New York, and myself.

Because of these efforts, Hawai'i and its governor were never again characterized as being fiscally irresponsible. Hawai'i retained its credit rating, having no real problem placing its bonds in the marketplace at competitive rates. The Mauna Kea Hotel development was completed, and the state started construction of the Kaahumanu highway from the Kona airport to the Kawaihae area, opening up the whole coastline as the Gold Coast for dynamic economic development.

Indeed, Hawai'i was changing as outside corporations and investors helped diminish the control of the Big Five over the island economy. Many local companies simultaneously rose in prominence. Changes also came to the Big Five corporations from within, as more of them became public companies— gradually, the *kamaaina* family control slipped to new public ownership outside Hawai'i. Moreover, greater racial democracy began to affect the islands' legal and business communities. The racial makeup of the judiciary changed as more non-white lawyers were appointed by the elected governor. In turn, these changes affected matters beyond the courtroom, such as the appointment of trustees of the Bishop Estate. Private clubs such as the Pacific Club and Oahu Country Club, which had historically restricted their membership to whites, now opened their doors to local non-whites. The rapid changes in the political, economic, financial, and social landscape that took place during these three decades completely undermined the prewar oligarchic plantation system of the Big Five.

Recent historical reviews of these dramatic years have suggested that this liberalization of Hawai'i had a darker design and motive. For example, *Land and Power in Hawai'i* by George Cooper and Gavan Daws paints an ugly picture of the collusion between political power and land use that was allegedly tied in with personal gain. This study implies that there was a conflict of interest in many cases, and it questions the ethical standards of people in positions of power. While the authors do not argue that any illegalities took place, they suggest the misuse or abuse of power.

The ultimate ethical issue is not whether people in politics should be denied opportunities to enhance personal economic interests or investment possibilities. The concept of a democratic government in a free society is dependent on private citizens who, though they are engaged in the marketplace to make a living, are willing for a period of time to enter public service. There will always be a natural relationship between political power and private-sector benefits. When an individual is engaged in both activities simultaneously, the true ethical issue should focus on that particular person's alleged misuse of government funds or breach of rules for personal gain. It appears that the criticism against the politicians/entrepreneurs of our generation is that we totally altered the political and economic landscape and rapidly expanded and opened the economy for everyone—everyone benefited from those changes. The implication that the political process was abused for personal gain is based on certain out-of-context facts and statistical data. These data are easily used for criticism—especially by academics or media reporters, who try to wear a halo on their heads but are themselves rarely involved actively in any risk-taking process in either the private or public sector. These same critics have little understanding of the socioeconomic stranglehold that an entire generation of islanders suffered under when "land and politics" were truly in the hands of the few.

After being freed from the glass house of elective politics, I could enjoy the privacy of my law practice and business affairs while helping the governor as a private citizen whenever asked. When my friend, Bert Kobayashi, accepted the appointment to the Hawai'i Supreme Court, a vacancy opened for attorney general. Fortunately, I was able to persuade the governor that I could be more helpful to his administration as an outsider than as an insider. I was not appointed attorney general and continued my private life, busy with my practice.

During Jack Burns' campaign for his third reelection as governor in 1970, I took time to help him in whatever capacity I could. After his victory, I knew this was going to be his final term. As a result, I had hoped this campaign would also be the last time I would be heavily involved in fund-raising, controlling the financial outlay, and coordinating the organizational activities of a major campaign. One morning in 1972, the governor invited me to breakfast. Usually at these meetings he would want to hear about certain people I knew, or learn my impressions about certain business groups or other relevant matters of the day. However, this particular morning he mentioned that a search was going on for someone to fill a trustee position at the Bishop Estate. I said that I had not given any thought about the trusteeship and he would be foolhardy to think about someone like me. I promised him that I would make a list of people he might recommend and would get back to him later.

I went back to my business without giving the matter any more thought. On my return from a mainland business trip, my secretary told me that there was a message from Supreme Court Chief Justice William S. Richardson. When I called him back, he asked me whether I was free the next night to meet with him and Bert Kobayashi.

Bert and I met at Bill's home in Manoa. The meeting started off with Bill informing me that I was the only person the whole court could agree upon to appoint as trustee of the Bishop Estate. I was incredulous and asked whether they considered the possible reaction of the Hawaiian community. I was a nisei, I reminded them, a fact that would not sit well with Hawaiians. Every one of my enemies would yell "politics," knowing my relationship with the Supreme Court and the governor. I tried to persuade them to reconsider, reiterating that I had not applied for the position and that there must be many more qualified candidates. I was doing well in my law practice and was deeply involved in some exciting investments. In addition, they were asking that I cut my relationship with Chinn Ho because of the appearance of conflict of interest.

"How much does a trustee earn?" I then asked. The figure was quite a bit less than what I was earning in my practice.

Bert then intervened, saying, "Don't tell me about the financial sacrifice you will be making. Remember the sermon you and the governor gave me about public service? You knew I was making a big financial sacrifice when I became attorney general."

I lost this battle with him. I finally agreed to accept the appointment. However, I told them I would need about two months to clear my desk of pending matters. I also would need to call Chinn, who was in Hong Kong, to tell him about the unwritten condition of my appointment. We knew that my selection would be controversial, but that evening none of us could have anticipated the intensity of the firestorm that would be ignited when my appointment to the Estate was made public.

CHAPTER FIVE

The Nisei Trustee of the Bishop Estate

THE FORMAL ANNOUNCEMENT of my appointment as trustee of the Bishop Estate came as a complete surprise to the community. I had not been suggested as one of the probable candidates in the rumor mill, and interested parties knew I did not solicit appointment to the position. Since the appointment that immediately preceded mine had been of a businessman of Chinese ancestry, the choice of another non-Hawaiian to the Estate, particularly a nisei, was almost unthinkable. My personal friendships with several of the justices on the Supreme Court was also no secret, nor was the fact that I was engaged in private law practice with interests in the corporate and real estate sectors. As a close ally of the governor who had turned down an appointment to be the attorney general of Hawai'i, my critics easily could level the charge of "cronyism."

While we expected some negative reaction to my appointment, none of us anticipated the intense bitterness and sometimes open and widespread hostility generated in the Hawaiian community, as political and racial considerations became mixed. The media fueled the fire with biased sensationalism in their reporting. The climate of confrontation was unprecedented as conservative, moderate, and young activist Hawaiians almost unanimously spoke out against my appointment. Understandably, they preferred someone of their own race to help run the Hawaiian institution that managed vast estates for the benefit of the Kamehameha Schools, the only private school for Native Hawaiian children.

The reaction would probably have been more subdued if a *kamaaina haole* had been appointed, since this would be in keeping with previous appointments. Even the appointment of another person of Chinese ancestry with business qualifications would not have generated such organized hostility and bitterness among most of the Hawaiian community. However, a lawyer of second-generation Japanese ancestry, without a family history, who had climbed the ladder to become one of the "newly arrived" on Hawai'i's economic and political scene, was a different story. Portrayed in the media as a political hack who allegedly abused political power for personal gain, I was considered an unacceptable choice to be a Bishop Estate trustee.

The focal point of the organized resistance rose out of Kawaiahao church and the Reverend Abraham Akaka. A church with roots going back to the original Protestant missionaries from New England and Hawaiian *alii*, including Bernice Pauahi Bishop, benefactress of the Estate, Kawaiahao was the preeminent and most tradition-bound church in Hawai'i. For generations the powerful *kamaaina haole* and their families met there with the Hawaiian *alii* and their families to pray. Kawaiahao seemed like the natural site where Hawaiians could gather together to fight this appointment—an appointment considered to be an insult to their community. The bells of Kawaiahao Church rang as Hawaiians marched around the statute of King Kamehameha protesting my appointment. The church was made available as a place for Hawaiian leaders to meet and plan their resistance. They filed suit in court to invalidate the appointment; many of my old political adversaries joined this litigation as lawyers.

I was badgered by the media and others everywhere I went. The justices of the Supreme Court and the governor were also subject to some of these same indignities. Looking back on this unhappy period, I can still remember the mixed emotions I felt as the recipient of stinging personal assaults on my character. My youngest daughter, at the time a high school student, was drawn into this storm of controversy, scorn, and bitterness. One day after she had learned that the position of trustee paid less than what I was asked to give up, she simply asked me, "Why?" The whole ugly situation made no sense to her, especially in economic terms. We were comfortably situated in Waialae-Kahala, enjoying the privacy of being out of politics. Why was it necessary, she asked, to go back into the fray when I was seemingly not wanted by those who were the beneficiaries of the Estate?

I could only explain to her that there are certain obligations you owe to friends who have stuck their necks out for you. They may be asking you to make a personal economic sacrifice, but they are also asking you to contribute to the broader community of Hawai'i. Again, values such as loyalty and obligation to friends, family, and community are important attributes we were taught to honor and respect. Why else had we been willing to make the sacrifices required of us during World War II unless it was to heed these voices of duty and obligation?

Fortunately, my daughter understood. She stood by silently and stoically with me, as did my wife and other children. Then there were the death threats. When these cowardly threats were made against me, I viewed them as irrational, emotional outbursts. However, one early morning, while it was still dark, my daughter answered the phone. The caller threatened her life and the lives of my wife and other children unless I quit. The situation had become completely unacceptable and ugly. We moved to one wing of the Ilikai Hotel with full-time security. My appointment had now become a family matter. My wife and children reassured me that they would not back down. Though the experience was unnerving, we were strengthened as a family. Fortunately, none of these threats materialized and finally the veiled, cowardly calls ceased.

Despite these negative, unhappy experiences, I was uplifted by friends who stood up against the tide of loud and intense opposition. From my friends in the Hawaiian community came several letters of support, expressing their belief that I would greatly benefit the Bishop Estate and the Kamehameha Schools. Veterans of the 442nd and 100th Battalion who were incensed by the anti-nisei racial undertones also rallied to my support. They stood resolutely behind me—although, at my request, quietly. Facing the ire of many critics over this issue, Governor Burns responded calmly and reasonably to every letter he received, explaining why he believed my appointment would benefit the Estate. All these expressions of loyalty and support somewhat eased my pain and hurt. I wrote to the friends who stood by me, expressing my commitment to them.

I was determined to keep silent in public. I had learned during my years in public service to avoid the press as much as possible. After all, I had no reason to believe I would be treated fairly or rationally. "Journalistic integrity" was but convenient rhetoric. Having deadlines to meet and seeking out sensational news, journalists often include inaccuracies and hyperbole in their stories. I therefore tried to maintain as low a profile as I could. Like everything else, I repeated to myself, this too would pass. In another month, a new media controversy would take the place of the Takabuki story. The justices stood by their selection, and so did I. The courts validated my appointment, and I started my tenure as trustee of the Bishop Estate on August 1, 1972, with mandatory retirement at age seventy.

Six months after the storm over my appointment had subsided, my personal friend, David Trask, who was then president of the Hawaiian Civic Club, asked me to address the organization at its state convention in Honolulu. "Give me a few days to think about it," I told David. I then called a few friends whose views I respected for advice. They all encouraged me to take this opportunity to speak to a statewide Hawaiian organization. By then a more reasonable picture of who I was and the kind of work I was doing for the Estate had filtered into the Hawaiian community. I was also participating in many meetings with young activist Hawaiians to discuss their concerns and what the Bishop Estate could and could not do. We had many dialogues on what I was doing with the other trustees in conducting the business of the Estate and schools. Consequently, I decided the time seemed right to make a public statement to the Hawaiian community regarding my new role as a trustee of the Bishop Estate.

The underlying thrust of my address was my total commitment to do the best possible job as a trustee, utilizing whatever knowledge, talent, and experience I had. I expressed my hope that the *keiki o ka aina* of various ethnicities have the same mission to contribute to a common cause of a better Hawai'i, all within the warm Polynesian tradition. The Hawaiians, I said, were ultimately responsible for establishing their own goals and achieving their own hopes and aspirations, as only they could speak as the indigenous people of Hawai'i. The audience gave me a standing ovation, although I was not sure how much of it was out of a sense of Hawaiian politeness. From that time on, I believed I was accepted as a trustee by the Hawaiian community because of what I was trying to do—to do my best with whatever talent I had for the Estate.

The Hawaiian Civic Club speech was an extremely important statement that publicly expressed my personal commitment as a nisei to the mission of Bishop Estate. The 1970s were a watershed in Hawai'i's multicultural relations. Many ethnic groups were rediscovering their heritage and reaffirming their cultural values, which stimulated their agitation for more political and social empowerment. In many ways my appointment precipitated the activist movement of the "Hawaiian Renaissance," as many native voices cried out unmistakably that there had to be qualified Hawaiians who could serve as trustees of this basically Hawaiian institution. Ever since my appointment, this desire and need of the Hawaiians has dictated the appointive process for trustees by the Supreme Court justices. All five trustees after my appointment were of Hawaiian ancestry. While it is not mandatory that a trustee be Hawaiian, with everything being equal, preference should be given to those who can trace their lineage to Hawaiian ancestors.

I realized from the beginning that my role as trustee would always be low-key. Collectively, we named Dick Lyman, the only part-Hawaiian during my early tenure, as chairman of the board of trustees, a position he maintained until his death in 1988. Loved and respected by the community, Dick Lyman was a *kupuna*, or respected elder, in the finest sense of the word. Sensitive to the rising concerns of the Hawaiian community, he often helped the Estate work out problems that arose in the many different segments of the Hawaiian community. We got to be good friends, and I stood at his side many times in communicating with the Hawaiian groups on what the Estate was doing to generate more revenues. He was the facilitator while I was the technician—a team that worked well together.

One of my first tasks as trustee was to compile a clear picture of the portfolio of assets of the institution. I was surprised by the lack of coordinated information provided to the trustees—the information we needed to make decisions. With limited funds available for staff, this situation was understandable. The Estate was therefore projecting the next year's budget based on the previous year's budget. Income revenues were insufficient to meet the expenses of the Estate and schools, and a plan approved by the Internal Revenue Service was in place to sell undeveloped land to cover the costs of these ongoing expenses. The Estate was a classic case of being land-rich but cash-poor.

To get an overall view of the past, I first requested an executive summary report of audited revenues and expenses for the previous five years. None was available. To expedite the process and since I knew what I wanted, my secretary and I prepared this report ourselves based on annual audits. Next, I wanted a budget analysis of revenues and expenses for at least the next three years. Since the sales of land approved by the IRS had not yet taken place, it was necessary to calculate this three-year projection using assumptions from a number of different scenarios, calculating the income derived from each scenario, and determining how this income affected the future budgetary needs of the schools and the Estate. Years before, when we were analyzing business ventures at Capital Investment, I had Donald Wong, chief financial officer at Capital, crunch numbers based on various assumptions and options. This process of evaluation was relatively new at the Estate, where financial projections had been either loosely prepared or unavailable, making judgment calls difficult.

Number-crunching was minimal. The staff was more operationally oriented rather than financially oriented.

Eventually I developed my own financial projections based on certain economically feasible assumptions. At the time, a major sale of Kapua was being negotiated. Kapua was an *ahupuaa*, or Hawaiian land area starting from the mountains and going to the ocean, consisting of 15,000 acres located on remote undeveloped volcanic lands on the island of Hawai'i. The buyer saw potential in growing macadamia, a long-term agricultural use, and a remote possibility of using the oceanfront lands for second home residential development. Our report showed a geological fault on the property and the possibility of volcanic eruption on the site. We therefore sold it. When the buyer had a difficult time meeting the terms of our sales agreement, we restructured the agreement. We ended up restructuring the agreement several times, negotiating a floating interest rate based on the prime rate. The floating interest rate at one point reached over 20 percent per annum. We made out extremely well when we finally collected the principal and interest on this sale years later.

While these IRS-approved sales of undeveloped lands, mostly on the island of Hawai'i, had little impact on the total value of the Estate's land portfolio, it was not economical to use the corpus of the Estate to meet operating expenses. If this trend continued, the corpus would eventually be reduced, affecting the long-term survival of the Estate. While this was going on, however, some growth of revenue was taking place as the lease for the Sheraton Waikiki Hotel was renegotiated; leases in the Kapalama industrial area began to generate income; and the residential leasehold lots in Hawai'i Kai and the Windward and Leeward areas began to generate income as well. This increase in revenues, together with the sale of lands, was adequate to meet the operating expenses of the Estate and schools. But growth was slow.

As a charitable, tax-exempt entity, the Estate was severely restricted by the Internal Revenue Code in developing its landholdings, which constituted most of its assets. In order for the Estate's land revenue to be tax-exempt, the revenue had to be passive rental income. Revenues raised by using debt to improve the land were taxable. The Estate was also prohibited from developing or selling residential lots. Such activities would position it in the real estate business, generating unrelated taxable business income. For this reason, the Estate's development of raw land was initiated through leases to developers, who subdivided the land, constructed the infrastructure, and sold houses and lots to consumers along with long-term leases from the Estate. Lease rental income was passive, tax-exempt revenue. Bishop Estate, as a charitable entity, had to use this development structure of leasing its undeveloped land to third-party developers to generate tax-exempt lease rentals.

To make these developed lots marketable, the FHA and other lending institutions required that the fixed lease rent period exceeded the mortgage term. To create affordable housing for low-income families, the Estate set a low, fixed rent for a period of forty years in several instances. Ironically, these leases, which were originally created to meet the need for affordable housing, had a substantial negative impact on the value of the Estate's interest in the leasehold. The low lease payments for a fixed period had the unintended result of lowering the appraisal value of the lessor's leasehold interest. Thus, the lease-to-fee conversion law adopted decades later unexpectedly and substantially reduced the appraised value of the Estate's interests. This gave a windfall to the lessees at the expense of the Estate and was palpably unfair. While there is a public policy to support residential fee simple ownership, it seems that fairness would dictate balancing the comparative equities of lessors and lessees using the historical context in which these leases were made. All of the leases were made at a time when a lease-to-fee conversion law was never contemplated by either party. However, this balancing was not to be. The highest court of the land has held that the lease-to-fee conversion law is constitutional and therefore landowners can be forced by law to sell their leasehold and reversionary interests to lessees based on the current appraisal value of the lessor's interest.

Charitable landowners do benefit in one way: lease-to-fee conversion by eminent domain makes revenue from sale of their property tax-exempt. Forced conversion of the Estate's leasehold and fee interests in single-family residential lots resulted in substantial amounts of tax-exempt income. Much of the Estate's corpus, which had traditionally been land, was now cash. Prudent redevelopment and diversification of this cash principal into higher-earning financial assets and real estate became the next order of business for the Estate. The transition from a portfolio of basically a single Hawaiian asset—land—to a multifaceted investment portfolio with real estate and financial assets outside Hawai'i was about to take place.

Compared to many other national charitable trusts, the Estate was in a unique situation with its land-based assets. This was made dramatically clear to me when I became acquainted with the asset manager of the Duke University portfolio. Duke was joining us in advocating certain changes in the Internal Revenue Code. These changes would allow educational institutions to continue to have certain tax-exempt income even if they used debt to develop the land from which the income is generated. Under the law as it existed, income generated from any asset, including real estate, which was encumbered with debt, caused such income, including passive rental income, to be taxable. But unlike financial assets, real estate required substantial capital to develop, normally with long-term debt. Making real estate improvements on a cash basis placed a heavy burden on the landowner—so much so, that it was almost impossible to do. Congress had earlier removed pension funds from this debt-financed restriction. Now, we were asking for an extension of this exception to include educational institutions. The revenue impact of such an exception to the nation's fiscal policy was not significant. The impact on the Estate, however, with its large landholdings, was significant. Such an exception would allow the Estate greater flexibility to develop and improve its land for investment purposes. With the use of debt, the Estate could develop and redevelop its land for commercial, industrial, and residential use and it could leverage real property investment purchases. Understandably, then, the Bishop Estate led the effort among educational institutions to pass this amendment to the tax code in Congress. Senator Matsunaga, carrying our proposal to the joint tax conference committee of Congress, finally secured passage. This debt-financing amendment became an economic prop for the future development and expansion of the Estate's real estate holdings.

The asset manager of Duke University visited Honolulu with the school's basketball team, which came to compete in the University of Hawai'i's Rainbow Classic. He took time to meet the trustees at our biweekly board meeting. He described how Duke University was deploying its portfolio primarily in financial assets of stocks and bonds. Knowing that the Bishop Estate's portfolio was basically land, he remarked about the differences in investment strategy between our two institutions. He noted that what was traditional investment to his institution was not traditional to us (stocks and bonds), and what was traditional to us was untraditional to them (land).

However, a transition was beginning within the Estate. It needed to redeploy and diversify its investment portfolio into financial assets and real estate outside Hawai'i. There were many reasons for this. The Estate was being punished by politics that favored lessees. Governmental and administrative red tape made development of Estate lands difficult and stifling, and opportunities for financial asset investment in the islands were, at best, limited.

Just as we were becoming involved in this transition, the state advised us that our office at Halakauwila Street was going to be condemned to facilitate the construction of the state judiciary building. A search began for the location of our new office. It finally came down to a choice between a single-purpose building at the Kapalama Heights site on the school campus and the multipurpose Kawaiahao Plaza building located across from Honolulu City Hall at the head of the Estate's Kakaako lands. Developers of the Kawaiahao Plaza initially wanted the Estate as a major lessee of the building, but I explicitly told them that we were not interested in leasing space. If we were to relocate to Kawaiahao, we would be interested in acquiring the property. Without a major tenant like the Estate, the project was in trouble. A reasonable price was negotiated and four of the five trustees agreed to acquire Kawaiahao Plaza, viewing it as a more desirable site than the single-purpose building on the school campus.

One trustee who disagreed with the acquisition brought suit primarily against me, calling the other trustees incompetent for following my recommendation. I decided to confront him on a one-on-one basis. The resulting lawsuit created a difficult period for the Estate, with the staff caught in the middle of the controversy. The suit personally cost me a substantial sum of money for legal costs and attorney fees, as well as my time as a litigant and the time of the other trustees and staff. This lawsuit showed that trustees, as fiduciaries, are exposed to personal risk and could lose substantial amounts of personal funds in suits like these. The purchase of Kawaiahao Plaza was upheld by the courts and the Bishop Estate still owns it today. The building not only houses the original staff, which moved in when we acquired the building, but also accommodates the later substantial expansion of Estate personnel. In addition, the value of the land and building more than quadrupled in about four years from date of purchase.

Development of the Royal Hawaiian Shopping Center on the six acres fronting the Sheraton Waikiki and Royal Hawaiian Hotels reflected another fundamental change at the Estate. As explained before, tax laws caused rental income from debt-financed improvements to the land to be taxable. The Bishop Estate did not have the cash to develop the shopping center so it was necessary to borrow funds. But debt made the rental revenues from the center taxable. So, the development was done through a taxable subsidiary of the Estate. This project made economic sense as a long-term investment undertaken through a wholly owned taxable subsidiary. The after-tax income of the subsidiary, which would be declared as dividends to the Estate, would be tax-exempt. As discussed previously, we were eventually able to amend the Internal Revenue Code, allowing the Estate to own the shopping center directly with debt without adverse tax consequences.

The change in the tax laws also allowed the Estate to acquire other projects, such as the Windward Mall. So too, with
the Estate's investment in Las Vegas apartments, which gen-
erates rental income. Besides such rental income, the Estate
could now also earn additional passive tax-exempt income
through arbitrage. The Estate could use its good credit rating
to procure financing at a lower interest rate than others. The
Estate could then offer to finance an investment by offering a
loan at the less favorable market rate available to its partners,
while obtaining financing at its preferred rate. The difference,
or spread, could now be taken as tax-exempt income by the
Estate.

Based on the Estate's high credit rating by the national rating agencies, the Estate could obtain funds at a favorable interest rate. It was also able to issue its own commercial paper.
These factors allowed the Estate to leverage its investments
and engage in arbitrage opportunities. The new debt-finance
tax law for real estate allowed the Estate to use low-cost debt
for improving or buying investment properties, and thereby
maximize the use of its financial power and strength for opti-
mum returns on its investment. This use of credit, creative
financial structuring adjusted to the needs of particular real
estate investments, and arbitrage of different rates in the
market were valuable lessons learned from my days with
Sam Silverman.

Real estate investments by the Estate outside Hawai'i
included participation in shopping centers in Milwaukee
and near San Francisco; residential, industrial, and commercial projects near Washington, D.C., Raleigh-Durham, and
Atlanta; and apartments in Las Vegas, Denver, Orlando, and
Palm Beach. The acquisition of the timberlands in Upper
Michigan, a land area even greater than our total acreage in
Hawai'i, was initially structured with debt. Eventually, this
deal was restructured and the Estate's half interest went to
full ownership of these lands. As in Hawai'i, these land values
will only increase over time. If the Estate is patient, these land
investments should be very rewarding in the future.

Outside Hawai'i, the Estate's real estate investments are passive. The Estate takes a limited partnership interest in partnerships with local real estate professionals who share risks with the Estate. The Estate usually receives a preferred return on the invested capital before the managing partnership gets a percentage of the profits. Real estate is a highly local activity, best performed by those individuals who know the area, its market, its politics, and the lenders. An outsider without a local connection who invests is asking for trouble. In this type of real estate investment, you must have an exit strategy based on computation of an internal rate of return on the investment at the end of ten years. These land investments are not structured to be held in perpetuity, unlike real estate in Hawai'i.

Real estate in Hawai'i is still the most important asset of the Estate. It is the core of its investment portfolio, including investment properties like Royal Hawaiian Shopping Center, Windward Mall, the Towne Center in Hawai'i Kai, office buildings in Waimalu and Waiakamilo, Kawaiahao Plaza, industrial properties in Waiakamilo and Kakaako, and other smaller income-producing properties. Leases are beginning to generate significant commercial rentals from Kahala Mall, Pearlridge Shopping Center, Kamehameha Shopping Center, and resort rentals like the Sheraton Waikiki, Royal Hawaiian, and Kahala Hilton. Matured industrial leases renegotiated after the initial rental period in Kakaako and Kapalama; commercial and apartment leases in smaller areas in Kaheka and Moiliili; and other higher land uses in urban Honolulu, the Leeward and Windward areas on Oahu, are now generating significant lease rentals. These Hawai'i real estate transactions are conducted by the Estate very differently from properties located in the continental United States. We have staff here to manage our real estate. Since we know the market and the political landscape, we expect to hold the land in perpetuity whenever possible. We have our wholly owned subsidiary to manage the Estate's commercial properties. As the insiders, we know Hawai'i. We also honor the provision of Bernice

Pauahi Bishop's will to keep the real property unless the best interest of the Estate dictates otherwise. In fact, the Estate may add additional Hawaiian property to its assets in the future when the purchase of such lands makes economic sense.

Looking forward, the economic future bodes well for the Estate. In time, when the leases on urban lands expire, the Estate has the management capability and available resources to take over and operate such shopping centers, commercial office buildings, and industrial properties. The Estate's capacity and patience to redevelop its properties for high uses in Kakaako, and later in Kapalama, constitute a sound long-term policy. Since the Estate owns the land, it can afford to be patient. The new debt-financing law allows the Estate to issue short-term commercial paper at a low cost, or to procure intermediate or long-term financing with established lenders as needed at the most favorable rate available. The high credit rating Bishop Estate enjoys with the national rating bureaus like Moody's and Standard & Poor's allows easy access to the credit market. The Bishop Estate can only become bigger and stronger in the future.

Land banking in rural Oahu and the neighbor islands will create the basis for future value as Hawai'i grows in those areas. A good example is the Keauhou Shopping Center in Kona on the Big Island, which will someday meet our expectations as Kamehameha Investment Company, the wholly owned taxable subsidiary, slowly turns the Keauhou area around. The shopping center is guided by a management team that recognizes that the center will eventually grow as the area grows. KTA Supermarket and Longs Drug Store are major tenants that give the Keauhou Shopping Center stability and long-range growth. With strategic, long-term investment, the Estate is big enough and has a sufficiently deep pocket to work a turnaround. With time as its ally, the Estate can be patient as eventual growth adds to the value of the surrounding area it owns.

Although real estate is the most important asset base of the Estate's trust corpus, land is not the only investment asset in any investment portfolio. Other assets are available in the marketplace. A prudent investment program calls for asset allocation with various kinds of assets to balance a portfolio. A national investment consultant, Cambridge Associates, which advises many major educational institutions on traditional investments in marketable securities and financial assets, was retained to assist us in redeploying part of the sales proceeds of the leasehold conversions into financial assets outside Hawai'i. Private placements in financial assets began in earnest in conjunction with other tax-exempt institutions. These investments were structured by investment banking firms on Wall Street.

We started slowly, following institutions like Duke and the advice of investment consultants. Since I had negotiated financing arrangements with New York money market banks and insurance companies for Hawai'i developments before, I was no novice to the Wall Street culture. I had walked the streets of New York City with Chinn Ho and Sam Silverman many years before. Even though investment banking differs somewhat from loan negotiations, the setting was still Wall Street. In one way or another, the Estate had become involved with most of the investment banking firms in New York for its private placements of investments. Some of these investment opportunities stemmed from my personal relationships with some of New York's leading players. For example, since I was an old friend of the CEO of the Rockefeller group, we were invited to invest with that major institution. Goldman Sachs was our primary investment banker. The investment banking arm of J. P. Morgan Bank was a partner in Centre Re Insurance Company located in Bermuda. Kemper Insurance Company, Guy Carpenter, a subsidiary of Marsh & McLennan, Northwestern Life Insurance, and Zurich Life Insurance of Switzerland were all players in the deal. I sat on the board of directors of Centre Re. In about three years, Zurich and other strategic investors in the insurance field wanted to buy the interest of the financial investors, like J. P. Morgan and the Estate. The Estate exited with a very substantial gain.

J. P. Morgan later introduced the Estate to another major investment opportunity in catastrophic insurance, again located in Bermuda, with Marsh & McLennan and several other investment banking groups. The Estate took a share in the company similar to that of J. P. Morgan and Marsh & McLennan. I also sat on this company's board of directors. In less than a year, we made an initial public offering (IPO) of the company, trading first on NASDAQ and later on the New York Stock Exchange. All the investment partners now have marketable securities valued substantially over their invested capital.

The Estate invested in Saks Fifth Avenue with Invesco, a highly regarded private investment banking firm, and the legendary Saudi prince, Alwaleed Bin Talal Bin Abdulaziz Alsaud, who hit a home run in investing in Citicorp. This was an investment in a franchised name with exit through a public offering in the future. The Estate did well in this deal as well.

The Simon group, headed by investment guru William Simon, negotiated to buy a controlling interest in the American Security Bank (in Honolulu) from a Hong Kong group. They came to us for participation in this acquisition and we negotiated a position as the major financial investor in the deal. We later exited from this investment with a substantial gain, selling our interest to First Hawaiian Bank. This affiliation created the opportunity to later participate as the American component of the People's Republic of China's Xiamen International Bank.

Next came the acquisition of control of Honolulu Federal Savings and Loan Association ("HonFed"), the largest savings and loan in Hawai'i, which was in trouble due to large nonperforming real estate loans. The savings and loan was being scrutinized by federal regulators as being undercapitalized, with insolvency a real possibility. We were again asked to participate as the major financial investor by the Simon group. We negotiated and structured an even better participation than in the prior American Security Bank arrangement. With adequate capitalization, HonFed was turned around in a short period. Bank of America, long seeking an entry into Hawai'i, saw an opportunity to do so by buying HonFed. A sale was negotiated and we exited from the venture along with the Simon group.

Both of these private placements of local financial institutions were highly profitable, tax-exempt gains for the Estate.

Other smaller private placement investments in various stages of maturity were pursued. Although mismanagement and fraud caused some of these investments to turn sour, most were good with a few "home run" possibilities. We diversified our investments in reinsurance, hospitals, managed health care, retailing, banking, regional convenience stores, oil and natural gas, and research companies in science and technology to spread the risk exposure over a wide and diversified field. The Bishop Estate was now being recognized as one of the "big" players among tax-exempt institutions in the capital markets on Wall Street with a reputation for being knowledgeable and having the ability to move relatively quickly if necessary.

The most important investment in this financial asset field was in Goldman Sachs, the premier private investment bank on Wall Street. If there is one legacy I can point to with pride, it is the part I played in structuring this investment. Before we were invited to invest in Goldman Sachs, the Estate was already involved with them as participants in many private placements. They were our principal source for placing short-term and money market funds, assisting and advising us on securing a credit rating from the national credit rating of Moody's and Standard & Poor's so we could issue short-term commercial paper on Wall Street. Through these relationships, Goldman Sachs knew about the Estate and we knew about them. We had the highest rating available to a charitable institution—A-1+ and P-1 from Standard & Poor's and Moody's, respectively.

In early December 1991, I was in New York with Eric Martinson, a young executive from our financial asset section, meeting with the partners of some of the investment groups affiliated with the Estate. I received a call from Fred Steck, a vice president of Goldman Sachs in their San Francisco office. He asked whether I had some time to meet with him, a managing partner, and several other partners at their Wall Street headquarters. During the meeting, Jon Corzine, a partner on the senior managing committee of the firm and recently elected head of Goldman Sachs, along with several other partners, asked whether the Estate would have any interest in acquiring a partnership interest in Goldman Sachs with an investment of several hundred million dollars. That morning I had read in the *New York Times* that Goldman Sachs sold fixed-coupon long-term bonds of about $240 million to pension fund institutions.

"Yes," I answered recalling the morning article. "I think we would be interested, but in an equity interest, not the kind of bonds with a fixed-coupon rate I read about this morning." I said that it was also important to structure the investment as a tax-exempt transaction. Later that day I told Eric about this meeting with the Goldman people and how we needed to begin the due diligence process to evaluate the economics of this investment. We needed to study how to structure the deal as a tax-exempt transaction under the Internal Revenue Code. It was by far the largest single investment commitment ever to be considered by the trustees and I knew we would need to discuss the matter at the next board meeting in Honolulu.

In an executive session of the trustees, I went over what was discussed at the meeting and how much money we were being asked to place in this transaction. I told them I had given a lot of thought about the pros and cons of this deal over the weekend, and I was convinced we should take our best shot. This was an investment opportunity for immediate redeployment and diversification of our portfolio in various types of financial assets with highly competent, professional management. Goldman Sachs was involved in fixed income, equity, commodities, investment banking, and asset management. Through this one investment, we could diversify immediately and our interests would be allocated in these areas with oversight by professional management. As a partner of this firm, we would share not only in the promotional and management fees, but the profit allocated to the manager from many investment programs with which we were already involved.

I further explained that I was confident that we would be able to finance this investment and indicated conceptually how it could be done. I recommended that we indicate our interest and begin negotiations to see whether a mutually satisfactory arrangement could be made. The trustees agreed, and I notified Goldman's point man, Fred Steck, of our interest in trying to make a deal. We also began to gather information about the firm in order to start an intensive due diligence covering the economics and tax implications of the deal. We needed to negotiate precisely what interest in the firm our investment dollars would buy. Goldman Sachs' team headed by Jon Corzine came to Honolulu in mid-December for a preliminary meeting with the trustees. The meeting was basically a first-time discussion between the principals to commence preliminary negotiations on how we could arrange an investment as a passive partner. They flew from New York to Honolulu the night before, met the trustees in the morning, and left Honolulu to return to New York in the late afternoon on the same day. The due diligence process then began in earnest.

Mark McConaghy of Price Waterhouse headed our tax team along with our staff tax specialist, Gilbert Ishikawa. Mitch Gilbert and Eric Martinson were the number-crunchers. They had computer printouts containing all the information provided by Goldman Sachs. Nathan Aipa, our general counsel, headed our legal side. This small but very effective and talented team, honed by past experience in private placement investment analysis and structure, spearheaded the Estate's efforts. We crunched numbers with different assumptions; high, middle, and downside scenarios; rates of return on capital invested with different profit scenarios; before and after state and local taxes, and, in some instances, taxes on international and global transactions. We tried to cover all the variables affecting the viability of the investment. We had confidential audited statements, balance sheets, and profit and loss statements going back seven years, unaudited financial statements for the fiscal year ending in November, and a projection for the year to come. A variety of professionals were involved in the process as we enlisted our tax experts to assess the tax information, independent Wall Street consultants to help us evaluate the various strategies and tactics of Goldman Sachs, and technical and legal experts in the securities field to help us check the present status of the firm before the Securities and Exchange Commission. This was the informational foundation necessary to help us make an investment decision on what percentage of the firm should be allocated to the Estate in return for the capital invested, and whether that percentage would generate favorable current and future yield to the Estate. While the dollar amounts were huge, the methodology for judging this investment was the same. The trustees had to decide whether this investment was good for the Estate.

Within a relatively short time, we were advised by our tax counsel that the investment could not be structured as a tax-exempt transaction. Goldman Sachs' tax counsel agreed. The nature of an investment banking firm, which used debt to conduct its business, would not allow an investment in the firm to be tax-exempt. The parameters of investment therefore had to change. A close review of all relevant tax implications had to be carefully considered, determining how it would affect the yield of our investment. The real bottom line was whether this investment was viable. We did our after-tax analysis and concluded that the investment would make economic sense if we could procure a certain percentage of the firm. If this could be done, the investment would be good, particularly in the long term.

Negotiations proceeded, but on a different level and scale. Taxes would diminish the gains allocable to us in the partnership. This tax burden was the same for Goldman Sachs. The vehicle for this investment had to be one of our taxable subsidiaries. By using a subsidiary, the income would be taxable at a corporate level, but dividends from our subsidiary to the Estate, its parent, would continue to be tax-exempt. We were also pleased with Goldman's policy that the partners reinvest a portion of their gain each year in the partnership in order to maintain the percentage of their interest in the firm. This policy conformed with our overall strategy of obtaining good current yield plus an annual increase in the invested capital. This assured growth of the corpus and an increasing current yield as the corpus grew. The needs of today would be met with current yield while the growth of the principal corpus would take care of tomorrow. Since the investment in Goldman Sachs satisfied this need for current yield and our corpus growth strategy, it was good for the Estate.

To assist us in our review of this investment, Jon Corzine arranged to have us meet the Sumitomo people, who five years earlier had invested in Goldman Sachs as passive partners. While Sumitomo originally wanted to be a participating strategic partner, the federal government disapproved of such a role in a U.S. investment banking firm for a foreign company. If Sumitomo invested, it would have to be as a passive and not strategic investor, such as we were being offered. We were able to meet privately with the Sumitomo executives at their New York office. During the meeting, they shared their thoughts and told us how satisfied they were with their investment. The current yield, they explained, was good, and reinvestment of a portion of their gain into the firm had substantially increased their original invested capital. They confirmed our assessment of Goldman Sachs as a first-class investment banking firm. This early relationship with Sumitomo was to pay dividends later when we finalized our investment in Goldman Sachs and obtained Sumitomo's consent to use their attorneys for documentation of the transaction.

Negotiations continued as information and data were faxed back and forth. Telephone calls were going both ways as the general parameters of the deal were being drawn. Staff on each side continued to resolve boilerplate matters. I spoke periodically with Jon Corzine when staff members reached an impasse. One time when my wife, daughter, and I were in Riverside, California, visiting my sister-in-law, Fred Steck tracked me down. "It is necessary," he said, "that Jon speak to you." We arranged a meeting in Goldman's Los Angeles office with Jon and another partner flying into L.A. from New York and Fred Steck flying in from San Francisco. My daughter and I drove up to Los Angeles from Riverside. For several hours we met to get the negotiations back on track. After lunch, we each departed Los Angeles to our respective destinations.

As these negotiations continued, I became deeply involved in the Estate's growing interest in China. We had an opportunity to invest in the Xiamen International Bank venture and several other smaller joint ventures. To negotiate these investments, I had to go to Beijing. Nathan Aipa was designated to head our staff team to go to New York City to negotiate details with the Goldman Sachs' staff team. At about 3:00 one morning I was awakened in my room in the Sheraton Great Wall Hotel in Beijing by the ringing of the telephone. When I picked up the receiver, I heard the pleasant voice of Elisa Yadao, director of communications for Bishop Estate, saying, "Wake up call." Nathan got on the phone to say that the negotiating teams were hung up on several matters. I must have been on the phone for more than two hours, going over various detailed issues in dispute with the Goldman Sachs' negotiating team. While these issues were vexing and frustrating, as such detailed issues are, they were not "deal-breakers." The difficulties could be worked out. I explained to Nathan that he had the discretion to resolve these issues as he deemed best. These types of disputes are part of the micro-grinding out of details during the negotiation of a deal by staff lawyers, tax specialists, and financial analysts.

On my return to Honolulu, I had to go to Singapore to meet a Singapore Development Bank executive on a possible joint purchase of shares in a PRC company that owned a large block of shares in the Xiamen International Bank. A staff member accompanied me on the trip. While staying at the Shangri-La Hotel in Singapore, faxes were being sent from New York, San Francisco, and Hawai'i from both sides on the reconstructed projection numbers for Goldman Sachs for the following year. I considered the percentage of the firm that was being offered as too low based on these reconstructed numbers. If the percentage was cast in concrete, we were faced with a "deal-breaker." It was crunch time.

On my return flight from Singapore to Tokyo, I had about seven hours in the air. I was alone as the staff member was flying home via Seoul, Korea. I had the reconstructed numbers faxed to me and kept running them through my hand-held H-P 12 calculator. The fellow sitting next to me on the plane must have thought I was a "number nut." With a yellow pad and my calculator, I crunched the numbers for six and a half hours—all the way from Singapore to Tokyo. I worked the numbers on various assumptions and scenarios, finally constructing and correlating the relative interests of Goldman Sachs, Sumitomo, and the Bishop Estate into an acceptable formula. I also calculated the gains each party would have assuming a conservative projection based on what the respective interest would be after our investment in the partnership. I calculated the threshold interest we should have in this package, and that figure was higher than what was then on the table. I could defend my set of numbers and make it clear that our investment was viable for all the parties. Our invested capital would enhance the shared return for the three of us.

I faxed these numbers to our staff and to Goldman Sachs from Tokyo, explaining to Jon by phone how I arrived at these numbers. Understandably, his firm wanted Sumitomo's tacit approval and he would want to explain these numbers to them. We discussed the probable percentage of the firm we could obtain for our invested capital. When I returned from Tokyo, I was informed that two other items were still left dangling. Faxes and phone calls flew between New York and Honolulu. When those matters were finally settled and a percentage of the firm agreed on, the negotiations were complete. To demonstrate their good faith in our new partnership, Goldman Sachs set up a substantial scholarship program for students at Kamehameha Schools.

Before retiring from the Estate I envisioned another type of long-range investment vehicle to be put in place for the benefit of the Estate. For many years, Larry Landry of the McArthur Foundation, Gene McDonald of Duke University, Mike Patrick of the University of Texas, and I met informally to discuss our various investment strategies. We often shared our problems in using investment bankers to promote our private placements and the frustrations in not being at the forefront of initially evaluating investment opportunities. We were interested in finding an investment banking group to smoke out deals, analyze them, and present their analyses and findings for our review. That way our institutions could decide whether we wanted a part of the investment. Collectively we could not prudently establish a large enough funding commitment to attract established "deal-makers." However, we would be able to attract someone with a track record in smaller projects who might want to head our interest with a funding commitment from us. Broad investment criteria of risk and return would be established, incentives would be structured, and a relatively fast-moving process for considering investment would be set. Meanwhile, coverage of agreed operational costs to them would be assured by all of us. McArthur Foundation, Duke, and the Estate found a small investment banker and staff with a credible success record willing to risk their own capital to create a private investment banking firm. With the creation of this collaborative investment vehicle, our three nonprofit institutions now had an innovative means to consider private placement ventures firsthand.

Reviewing where Bishop Estate is today as a participant in private placement investments, it went from almost nothing to become one of the major institutional players on the national capital market. Although we may be small compared to many public and private pension funds, we march to a different drumbeat. The Estate needs to grow and prosper using what we have now, and cannot depend on a constant stream of contributions from employers and employees like those provided by pension funds. How well the Estate's corpus is preserved and how well it grows and appreciates determines how well it will support the educational mission intended by Princess Pauahi. Kamehameha Schools is the only and ultimate beneficiary of the Estate.

As the revenues of the trust substantially increased, the educational programs and facilities were expanded. The new

Midkiff Learning Center, a library with sophisticated computer hardware and software, a new chapel, a new cafeteria, a performing arts building, an athletic facility, renovation of the older auditorium and classrooms, have all been built to improve the educational facilities as a result of the Estate's financial growth. Many classrooms now have computers and science classes have needed laboratory equipment. The schools have the tools to teach the children under the guidance of a highly qualified faculty of professional educators. The enrollment in each class beginning at the seventh grade increases. Now one of the finest schools in Hawai'i, Kamehameha Schools should continue to improve in the future.

The educational mission of the Kamehameha Schools was as vital a part in my role as trustee as the achievement of financial stability and growth. Since I had begun my own college education in Teachers College, I viewed my job as trustee of a private school system as coming full circle in my career. Educated in the small rural public schools with limited facilities and resources, I never forget where I came from. One of my guiding tenets in education is that the rich and powerful do not really need our help, but the poor and weak do. This simple truth has served me well in evaluating new educational programs at the schools.

The Kamehameha Early Education Program (KEEP) fulfilled this goal of reaching out to young children who need help and would benefit the most from this educational program. A research program headed by teams of educators at the University of Hawai'i and the schools, KEEP addressed the educational problems of part-Hawaiian children in public schools in the poor, public housing districts of Kalihi in urban Honolulu. Situated in a public school environment, the program involved children in kindergarten through the third grade, exploring with them creative and innovative ways to enhance their learning and reading skills. The results of this innovative educational program have been nationally acclaimed for providing excellent research on the learning processes of children in economically disadvantaged districts. Because KEEP proved successful, Kamehameha Schools worked with the

State of Hawai'i's Department of Education using the program's findings to improve techniques for teaching in other comparable public school areas with large numbers of Hawaiian children, such as Nanakuli and Waianae. The program was a step forward in meeting the educational needs of all Hawaiian children and extended Princess Pauahi's legacy beyond the campus at Kapalama Heights.

Under the administration of President Jack Darvill, Kamehameha Schools attempted to enroll a more diverse Hawaiian student body. Recognizing that a selective admissions process was too restrictive, Darvill persuaded the trustees to change the admissions policy of the elementary school to a lottery system. Rather than employ selective admissions at the kindergarten level, by which admitted students were then assured a place in the schools until they graduated, all qualified Hawaiian children, not necessarily the brightest, would have an opportunity to gain an elementary education through an open lottery. For entry into seventh grade, a selective admissions process would be used as before and students from Kamehameha would have to compete with students from all other schools. Elementary students from Kamehameha would have no advantage over others in competing for a place in seventh grade.

The trustees adopted the recommendation of the administration because, for some of us, the opportunity to reach out to more youngsters, even if only for seven years, seemed worthwhile. In addition, the elementary education of Hawaiian children in general would be upgraded and improved through research and teaching methods learned from the early education program. For the first six years, as the first lottery group moved upward, the program continued without any serious problems. Parents of children who otherwise might not have qualified under the former selective system told us they were appreciative of the educational opportunity afforded to their children by the lottery system. They were frequently counseled that their children were not to be given automatic entry into the seventh grade, and parents were forewarned that some students would not qualify competitively for the higher level.

Despite all of these warnings and precautions, when many of Kamehameha's elementary students failed to be admitted based on competitive tests, the result for these students and their parents was traumatic. The experience of failure was considered demeaning and wrenching for both the students and their parents. There was a feeling that the schools did not do enough to prepare these students and that their failure to move on to the seventh grade tainted them as "inferior" or "stupid." Even in this highly charged, emotional climate, the trustees could not change the admissions policy at the seventh grade level to allow these children admission. Applicants from other schools had relied on the schools' representation that a selective admission process would be employed at the seventh-grade level and had chosen not to apply to Kamehameha for kindergarten.

The following year, the same disappointments and criticisms accompanied the seventh-grade selection process. Jack Darvill took early retirement and Michael Chun, a Kamehameha Schools graduate, was selected president after an extensive national search. After a great deal of soul-searching over this lottery system, and in consultation with others in the Hawaiian community, Chun and his administration recommended reversion to the former selective admission system at the kindergarten entry level. Once a child was accepted at Kamehameha Schools, that child could continue until graduation. The trauma of not being selected for seventh-grade entry was too great. The trustees adopted Chun's recommendation and reverted to the former selective system.

While the Estate had budgetary constraints, the trustees felt that it was also important to help Hawaiian students from public schools who sought higher education. As a member of a selection committee for a small private scholarship fund for part-Hawaiian students many years earlier, I vividly remembered the plight of a public high school graduate from Nanakuli who had wanted to be a teacher. While qualified to attend the University of Hawai'i, she could not do so without the assistance of a scholarship for her tuition. We provided the scholarship so that she could successfully enter the university with her tuition committed to her until she graduated. To assist other students in similar situations, I persuaded the trustees to set aside $25,000 for the Pauahi Scholarship of Kamehameha Schools to support post–high school education for public high school graduates of Hawaiian ancestry. These scholarships would be based on need. Today this fund has grown to $1 million and each year is used to assist eight hundred recipients who are primarily public high school graduates attending local universities and other post–high school institutions. The students also receive counseling services from Kamehameha Schools to help them successfully complete higher education. The Pauahi Scholarship of Kamehameha Schools is one more effort by our staff to work with public high school counselors to expand the legacy of Bernice Pauahi Bishop beyond the Kapalama campus. The scholarship will hopefully grow even more in future years.

In the early years, the curriculum of Kamehameha Schools was devoted to vocational training for the boys and domestic household preparation for the girls. Today that curriculum has evolved, transforming the schools into a college preparatory institution. While the industrial education and home economics programs have been retained, approximately 90 percent of Kamehameha School graduates now go on to college. The admission process remains selective. The schools provide high-quality education to Hawaiian children, thereby continuing to encourage excellence and provide role models for the Hawaiian community.

The one annual dinner I personally enjoy the most is the honor students dinner. At this annual banquet of students and parents, the graduating students with the highest grade point averages who participated in student activities are recognized. As the students' names are called out, the colleges where they have been accepted are also noted. Harvard, Yale, MIT, Stanford, and other major, highly rated educational institutions are frequently mentioned. The parents' pride shines throughout the dining room. My only concern is whether these talented Hawaiian youngsters will come home to Hawai'i after graduating from their respective universities. The type of professional and scientific opportunities suited to their talents may not be available in the islands, leading them to careers elsewhere in the United States. The displacement of these future professional "movers and shakers" from their home is one of the major problems that needs to be addressed in Hawai'i in the twenty-first century.

One of the immediate major challenges remaining before the Bishop Estate is expanding the educational mission to include more Hawaiian children. The present campus provides an educational opportunity to only about 6 percent of eligible beneficiaries. Only one out of ten applicants of Hawaiian lineage is accepted to the schools. Kamehameha Schools does not, and cannot, meet all the educational needs of the Hawaiian community. Most Hawaiian students, including the poorest and most educationally challenged, are in the public schools. Kamehameha Schools' off-campus extension program was an attempt to meet this need to expand. The schools have worked with the Department of Education (DOE) and other social agencies to start small, one-on-one programs to assist troubled teenagers. Neighbor island staff have been put together to meet the special needs of Hawaiian children on each island. While assisting the public school system with troubled Hawaiian youth has been a costly program if analyzed on a cost–benefit ratio, this effort by the schools is important in meeting the educational needs of the Hawaiian community. The schools also started the Vans of Hawaiiana program, in which vans are sent to public schools to expose all students to aspects of the indigenous Polynesian culture of Hawai'i.

The trustees have considered building another campus to expand the educational outreach. During my tenure on the board, it was felt that the capital expenditure and eventual operating costs of such a campus would strain the funding capacity of the Estate. We also studied the concept of building elementary schools in various parts of the state that would eventually feed students to the Kapalama campus for intermediate and high school. Again, the projected costs seemed to stretch the financial capacity of the Estate. There was also unexpected opposition to this plan from the DOE and the public school teachers, who felt threatened by this incursion of a private institution into public education. The current board of trustees is moving forward with the construction of new schools and as a result some of the partnerships with the DOE have been curtailed.

One area in which the DOE is not presently involved is preschool education, an educational niche that Kamehameha Schools sought to operate in. The needs of preschool Hawaiian children are very real and obvious and the opportunity exists to provide educational programs to these children so they will be motivated and prepared to enter kindergarten just as other children in private preschools. The current board has maintained its commitment to early education by working toward tripling enrollment in its preschools. The response to these efforts was and continues to be tremendous. Early results indicate that the preschoolers are provided important learning skills and that these skills carry over into kindergarten.

The admission policy of the schools gives preference to students of Hawaiian ancestry. This preference is not based on any blood quantum but on ancestral lineage. This policy has been attacked as a violation of the Civil Rights Act and on this basis critics have charged that the Estate's nonprofit tax exemption should be denied. The requirement of Hawaiian ancestry for admission was set by the initial group of trustees. The policy conformed to Princess Pauahi's intent to give educational opportunity to her Hawaiian people. Like other *alii* who bequeathed estates to help the aged, sick, and young, Princess Pauahi left her estate to help educate her people. For her troubled people, then as now, her legacy serves a definite need.

As long as there are more applicants than available openings at the schools, the admission policy will prefer applicants of Hawaiian ancestry. This racial preference passed the scrutiny of the Internal Revenue Service by a private letter ruling.

Hawaiians, as Native Americans, are specially classified like the other Native American Indian tribes and Aleuts by federal law. Therefore, educational and social programs can be geared to help and assist such disadvantaged groups. Not understanding the historical basis of this racial admission policy, or the continuing need for giving preference to a Native American group, a simplistic and unsympathetic treatment of this admissions program has appeared in the local and national media. Such shortsighted reporting is a disservice to the true intent of the Estate's benefactress to meet the ongoing educational needs and welfare of her people.

The requirement that the trustees and teachers of the Bishop Estate/Kamehameha Schools be Protestant is a religious policy detailed with precise instructions in Bernie Pauahi's will. Her specifications of religious affiliation reflected the attitudes of her times when there were sharp and sometimes bitter differences between Catholics and Protestants. This religious requirement continues to be challenged, although in the past the courts have upheld the policy because Kamehameha Schools is considered a religious educational institution. If in time this religious requirement is held to be against public policy, the impact upon the Estate of removing the religious restrictions will be minimal.

These problems of race and religion will no doubt continue to confront the educational mission of the Estate. However, the primary purpose of the Estate will continue to be the education of Hawaiian children, about one-fifth of whom will be "orphans and indigents of aboriginal blood." Since maintaining our tax-exempt status as an educational institution is essential, if at any time certain school practices jeopardize this status, adjustments will be made to preserve the Estate's primary educational mission.

As circumstances in the financial and social climate of Hawai'i change, priorities and policies may also change as new trustees in the future strive to achieve the institution's educational mission. They will deem what is proper and appropriate. Investment strategy for asset allocation may also shift. Kamehameha Schools is a living, viable institution that must adapt to the needs of society. While the educational mission will continue as mandated, the means of achieving this mission will be constantly reviewed, evaluated, and transformed as deemed appropriate by the trustees.

Takabuki *(far left, back row)* next to Richard Betsui *(far left, middle row)*, a teacher and YMCA counselor at Waialua High School. 1939.

Sergeant Matsuo Takabuki of the 442nd Combat Regiment Team, Camp Shelby, Mississippi. 1944.

Matsy and Ayako Takabuki return to Hawai'i on the *Lurline*. 1949.

The 442nd annual dinner is enjoyed by Takabuki *(center)* who was serving as president, and *(left to right)* Sam Sasai, Masato Doi, Ben Takayesu, Dr. Wallace Kawaoka, and Akira Fujiki. March 1952.

The members of the "Connally Caravan" (*front left to right:* Buck Buchwach, Matsuo Takabuki; *middle left to right:* Danny K. Meheula, Marian Kaipo; *back left to right:* Robert L. Stevenson, Frank Cockett) travel to protest the racial remarks about Hawai'i's people by Senator Tom Connally of Texas. The Caravan visited Austin, Texas, home of the 36th Infantry Division, and Washington, D.C. 1952.

Matsy Takabuki's favorite photograph when he ran for
the Board of Supervisors. Early 1960s.

Honolulu City Council (*left to right:* Clesson Chikasuye, Richard Kageyama, Ernest Heen, Herman Lemke, Noble Kauhane, Matsuo Takabuki, Masato Doi) are photographed with Honolulu Mayor Neal S. Blaisdell. 1961.

Matsy and Ayako Takabuki attend the inauguration of Governor John
Burns. 1962.

Takabuki attends Neal Blaisdell's sixtieth birthday celebration. 1962.

Mayor Neal Blaisdell *(second from the left)* and Takabuki survey the region of Panmunjon in South Korea as part of their army goodwill tour. They also traveled to Taiwan, Hong Kong, Naha (Okinawa), Hiroshima, and Tokyo. 1963.

Takabuki celebrates his inauguration to the City Council along with his wife Aya and children (*left to right:* Beth, Anne, and Glen). 1965.

The economic changes in Hawai'i during the 1950s and 1960s in tourism, construction, and real estate would be greatly influenced by island businessman Chinn Ho, his lawyer Matsy Takabuki, and New York financier Sam Silverman. During one of their many business trips together, Silverman *(far left)*, Ho *(second from the left)*, and Takabuki *(second from the right)* are pictured with a group of Asian businessmen. 1969.

Bishop Estate Trustee Richard Lyman and Trustee Takabuki are photographed during a thoughtful recess in estate business. 1988.

In Beijing, where Takabuki spoke at the Great Hall, he met Li Peng, Chinese premier of the National Government. 1991.

Matsy Takabuki's official Bishop Estate Trustee photograph. 1992.

Takabuki and Fumiaki Satake, a Japanese businessman and friend. Satake is from Shikoku, Japan, the home island of Takabuki's father.

Takabuki with Dennis M. Ogawa *(left)*, University of Hawai'i professor, and Sueaki Takaoka *(right)*, chairman of Seiyu Inc. Japan, a longtime friend and business associate. The occasion was to celebrate the fifth anniversary of Nippon Golden Network, which they were all instrumental in launching. 1987.

CHAPTER SIX

Toward the Pacific Rim Century

IT IS WIDELY recognized that the twenty-first century will be characterized by the emerging economic growth and leadership of the Pacific Rim nations. The greatest challenge for the United States, which is biased toward Europe, is to overcome the many cultural misconceptions that seem endemic to East–West relations. The American businessperson, who knowingly or unknowingly gives an impression of superiority by insisting on doing business his or her way, is usually courteously and gracefully stonewalled with ambiguous equivocation by his or her Asian counterpart. An American expects the person he or she is dealing with to be open and direct, but this does not usually happen in Asia. During discussions about the possibility of doing business together, the Asian may give the American a positive impression of agreement. However, in reality the response may actually be neither "yes" nor "no," but "maybe." As a consequence, those in the West who experience this hesitancy in giving a direct answer tend to believe that all the cards are not on the table. They view the Asian way of doing business as vacillating, indirect, and slow in arriving at a definitive understanding. Losing patience, Westerners often blow the deal. They fail to recognize that understanding and trust between the parties are necessary to create a long-term business relationship. To Asians, American businesspersons sometimes appear arrogant, and seem to be looking down on them as inferior and somewhat backward in their ways of doing international business. In fact, the record shows that the Asian entrepreneur is generally far more successful in conducting global trade than the American.

The variety of cross-cultural difficulties that businesses encounter in the international trade arena depends to some degree on size, technological know-how, and experience. Businesses that are multinational, such as IBM or Procter & Gamble, often conduct themselves with a sophistication that transcends cultural differences. When discussing business relations with multinational corporations such as Hitachi or Sony, the language of business crosses national boundaries. However, if the business level is on a smaller scale, the cultural and language differences often become more personalized and real. Unintentional misunderstanding and language miscommunication can often cause a breakdown of negotiations. To be successful at this level, an appreciation for, and understanding of, the multifaceted Asian businessperson are essential. One needs to be constantly on guard not to underestimate Asian counterparts who are usually smarter than may be at first assumed. As a trustee of the Bishop Estate, I constantly needed to remind myself that we were dealing in a different arena, an arena that required patience and understanding of Asian styles of doing business and an understanding of the various investment levels present in the Asian market, so different from our American market.

The difficulties Americans have in dealing with Asian companies became painfully obvious to me during my first personal involvement in negotiating with an Asian business entity. In 1959, I was asked by a local landowner to assist in negotiating a real property transaction in Honolulu with a major Japanese business conglomerate. The Japanese wanted to expand the company's operation to the United States and use the Honolulu site for a department store. An island businessman represented the Japanese interest and had approached the local landowner. I was asked to go with the CEO of the corporate landowner to Japan to assist him in the negotiations. That first trip to Japan turned out to be a real eye-opener.

During this trip, I soon experienced the cross-cultural differences that often arise in international business negotiations. The landowner wanted to lease the site to the Japanese. The Japanese, however, thought that the fee was available for purchase. The landowner made it clear that he would not sell the site, but would instead offer a long-term lease. The leasehold concept in Hawai'i was not the same as in Japan. Our real property law was based on English common law and Japanese law was based on German civil law. We have a tradition of long-term leases. They do not. The Japanese did not say "no" to our proposal to lease the site in Japan. They gave us the impression that they would consider it. In retrospect, I now realize that negotiations were doomed to fail from the beginning, but we were never directly given an answer until after we returned to Hawai'i.

While we failed to do a deal with that Japanese group in Hawai'i, they had started a department store in Los Angeles on land for which they acquired a fee. Once in L.A., the company made the same mistake that many Japanese businesses make in coming to the United States. They thought that since they were successful in Japan, they would be successful in the United States with a similar style of department store marketing. They found, however, that the American market, in terms of style, size, and goods, differed from the Japanese market. Failing to adjust to this difference, the department store eventually failed.

Even though my first business negotiations in Japan failed, I became deeply interested in Japan, its people and culture. After all, my parents had immigrated to Hawai'i from Japan, and my roots were there. Unfortunately, during that first business trip to Japan, I had little time for sightseeing, pursuing a busy schedule of business meetings and official dinners. One evening we were entertained by the president of our Japanese counterpart at a high-class teahouse in Akasaka, Tokyo. During the meal, one course was a fish called *ayu*, a delicacy that is broiled whole, without gutting. My *haole* friend looked at me with an expression on his face asking, "What are we going to do?" I responded, "We have to eat it." I knew it would be bad manners to decline. With our hosts, we ate the *ayu*, all of it, including portions of the innards. Holding the fish down was a memorable experience that helped me realize that I was indeed a cultural hybrid—an American with a Japanese face.

Through this and similar incidents, I discovered how Americanized most of the nisei had become and how little we knew about Japan. Of course, my fluency in Japanese at that time was very limited. In Hawai'i I had little opportunity to use Japanese except with my mother and at teahouses. I learned later to my chagrin that the Japanese we used was often the "old-fashioned" dialect of our immigrant parents. Once the mayor of Hiroshima City, who was visiting Honolulu to commemorate our sister-city relationship, laughingly told me that in Kauai with issei from Hiroshima, he heard the old, rural Hiroshima dialect of his youth. "It has been years since I have heard the old dialect spoken. Very rarely," he explained, "will you hear that dialect today in Hiroshima."

Fortunately, I had a bilingual younger brother, Ted, in Japan who was with the U.S. Military Interpreter Group. He graduated from Keio University with the help of the American GI Bill of Rights, and continued to live in Japan, marrying a Japanese national. I had not seen him for about two years. When he heard my Japanese, he laughed. I did not realize that I was speaking the old Hiroshima dialect used in Hawai'i rather than the conventional Japanese used in Tokyo. One time I got into a taxi cab with my brother. I told the driver that my hotel was "close" to the Akasaka Prince Hotel. For "close" I used the word *neki*. The cab driver looked at me puzzled while Ted laughed, correcting my dialect with appropriate conventional Japanese.

Years later, as I began to travel to Japan frequently, my Japanese slowly improved. In Honolulu, I practiced the language with Japanese hostesses at local bars and teahouses. Such establishments really serve two purposes—first they are settings for after-hours entertainment with Japanese friends, and, second, I could practice my Japanese. In Japan, I learned that the after–business hour entertainment was essential to develop and improve business relations. So when my Japanese friends or clients were in Hawai'i, I reciprocated by taking them to dinner and bars with Japanese-speaking hostesses.

Entertaining them in these bars, I had the chance to use and improve my language skills. The humorous side of this kind of learning is that many of us who honed our language in this fashion began speaking effeminate Japanese.

The next business project that brought me to Japan was in connection with the franchising of 7-Up. A client who had the 7-Up franchise in Okinawa was eager to extend it to the rest of Japan. The 7-Up franchise had worked well in Okinawa because the American military forces there knew 7-Up, which was the best-known U.S. lemon-lime soft drink. However, extending the franchise to the rest of Japan would prove to be very different. Unlike cola, which had no comparable Japanese product, 7-Up had to compete against Kirin Lemon, a popular Japanese lemon-lime soda that was sold by a major Japanese beverage company, which happened to have the largest market share of the beer industry. Kirin Lemon was already established with a whole distribution network. The 7-Up franchise would have to compete directly in this market against a large, established company with an inventory of various kinds of soft and alcoholic beverages.

Fortunately, we received great support from an Osaka businessman who liked 7-Up after tasting the product in the United States. He thought that 7-Up would sell well in Japan, particularly in the Osaka area. To back up his conviction, he made a substantial investment in the company, advising us first to buy land for our bottling plant in the Osaka area. A group of investors from Hawai'i also invested in this venture. American dollars were exchanged for Japanese yen. With an exchange rate of 360 yen for one U.S. dollar, we raised sufficient equity funds and invested capital in the project. While we had enough funds for some working capital, we needed a credit line from a local bank to conduct ongoing business. We were not highly leveraged, and our asset base of land and the bottling plant was significant.

Our application for credit was turned down by the very same Japanese bank that had gladly accepted our deposit of capital to fund the land and building, and which still held a balance in our account for operations. The bank told us that because we did not have any operating business history in Japan, they could not lend us the money. The Japanese bank was aware of our business plan and knew that we had paid for the land, the buildings, and the equipment. They also had more than adequate collateral to cover the loan. Although they were happy to take our deposits, a loan was out of the question because we had no actual record as an operating business. Doing business with a new company, particularly a foreign group, was not considered prudent banking practice, especially when that business would compete with a major commercial player in their district.

Of course, this situation is not unique to Japan. Any new business, especially one competing against a major established competitor who may have a relationship with the bank, would have trouble whether the bank was in Japan or in America. In the United States, however, a new company has a much easier time borrowing from a bank if it has credible references, a good business plan, and sufficient collateral to secure the loan. In Japan, and in Asia in general, the networks between local clients and banks are tighter, far more extensive and pervasive, and work against outsiders. We stopped doing business with that local Japanese bank. Instead, we established a banking relationship with the Japanese branch of a New York bank and established a credit line for the business with additional American guarantees.

In addition to the obvious banking problems and language difficulties in starting the 7-Up project, we faced an extremely complex distribution system made up of the manufacturer, wholesaler, and retailer. In the United States and Okinawa, distribution of soft drinks occurred from the manufacturer, who bottled the product and directly sold to the retailer through a driver-salesperson. For Japan, this arrangement was new and strange. Their conventional distribution system used a wholesale middleman who received the product from the manufacturer and then delivered it to the retailer. The wholesaler also provided credit and financing to the retailer, leading to tight interrelationships between the wholesaler and retailer. Japanese companies that sold products similar to 7-Up used this traditional Japanese distribution system of whole-saler and retailer. Progress in challenging this established dis-tribution system with a new and direct distribution system of the driver-salesperson was painfully slow and frustrating. Without demand for 7-Up by the consumer in the market-place and without credit to support the retailer from the com-pany, retail store space was not readily available. The prospect for sales growth was not encouraging.

Coca-Cola and Pepsi-Cola faced the same problem since they also used direct distribution as practiced in the United States. However, through extensive television advertising, these companies created public demand for their products. Since there was no comparable Japanese cola drink, con-sumers were asking for the product and retailers therefore had to carry the cola drinks. The direct distribution to retailers through the manufacturer's own driver-salesperson became acceptable practice for cola. In a short time, they expanded by selling their products in vending machines.

To be sure, the success that cola drinks, particularly Coca-Cola, enjoyed in Japan and globally is largely due to the fact that the parent company spent huge sums of money on adver-tising. Coca-Cola recognized that they had to create a demand for the new cola taste. Viewed as an investment in the future, they were not afraid to incur huge front-end costs to advertise and promote their product. Gradually, through advertising and promotion, they attracted young Japanese consumers to drink their new product and acquired name recognition through the media. The parent company of 7-Up, however, re-fused to underwrite this kind of front-end investment. With-out television advertising and promotion for a new product in a highly competitive field, 7-Up never really got off the ground like Coca-Cola. In our case, the land purchased by the company fortunately did appreciate enough to cover the oper-ating losses, but there was little gain to the foreign investors who got out.

Another good example of how American companies can succeed in Japan when they are willing to commit the front-end dollars for promotion is the experience of Kentucky Fried

Chicken. Even before McDonalds reached Japan, Kentucky Fried Chicken had name recognition among Japanese. One of the first American fast-food chains in Japan, KFC advertised extensively, riding the crest of Japanese curiosity regarding American products. It is never easy for any business to successfully enter a foreign market with a different language, business practices, governmental regulations and laws. However, if the company is patient and commits a long-term investment with expectation of early losses and deals realistically with the system in place, it has a chance to succeed.

My next trip to Japan in 1962 was not for business but was a goodwill trip in which I represented the Honolulu City Council. Mayor Neal Blaisdell asked me to accompany him to Hiroshima and Naha, Okinawa, to commemorate the establishment of sister-city relationships with those cities. Since many Japanese immigrants to Hawai'i had come from Hiroshima and Okinawa, this sister-city relationship was a very natural affiliation. The United States Army, which provided the transportation for this goodwill trip, expanded our itinerary beyond the sister-cities in Japan to other Asian nations. During the three-week journey, we visited many areas where U.S. troops were stationed, giving me the opportunity to see the U.S. presence in postwar Asia firsthand. We not only visited Okinawa, Hiroshima, and Tokyo, but Taipei, Hong Kong, and South Korea. The purpose of the trip was to cement goodwill between the Asian areas we visited and the United States, especially Hawai'i. We were also planting the seeds for future political, economic, and social relations with people in the Pacific Rim region. During our meetings with government and business leaders at various levels, we sensed that they had a genuine interest in Hawai'i. They informed us that since they had read so much about the beauty of the islands and knew that so many of Hawai'i's people had Asian roots, they wanted to visit Hawai'i. Travel between Hawai'i and Japan at that time was a grueling twenty-two hours by plane. The official exchange rate with Japan was 360 yen to one U.S. dollar, and there was an even worse exchange rate for the Taiwanese and Koreans. All of these countries had tight currency restrictions at the time. With all of these barriers, tourism to Hawai'i was still many years away.

My initial impressions of Asia were superficial. These visits were all prearranged with government and business leaders. However, what became clear to me as I traveled throughout the region was that the future of Hawai'i would be inextricably bound to these expanding Pacific Rim nations. With so many islanders having roots in these Asian nations, the opportunity to enhance our relations with Japan, China, Hong Kong, Taiwan, and Korea was becoming increasingly apparent. Indeed, the economic ties that would bind Hawai'i to Asia grew steadily in the next three decades. While the Japanese department store owners I first dealt with had failed to establish a branch store in Los Angeles, their pioneer effort to "internationalize" their market and expand their presence beyond Japan signaled dramatic changes in Japanese investments both throughout the United States and in Hawai'i.

As the Japanese economy grew, the yen appreciated against the dollar and the trade surplus began to favor Japan. The Japanese government encouraged recycling dollars by investing outside Japan, so Japanese investors began looking for investment opportunities in Hawai'i and the United States. Local retail companies such as McInerny and GEM were acquired from U.S. firms by Japanese companies and branches of Japanese retail stores opened in Hawai'i. Shirokiya, a Japanese retail firm, expanded to the islands. Local companies such as Holiday Mart sold their retail operations to Daiei, a large Japanese supermarket chain. Japanese investors also built hotels like the Hawaiian Regent. They acquired ITT's Sheraton Hotel. Ala Moana Center was jointly purchased by a Japanese company and a U.S. life insurance company and the Japanese eventually acquired the entire center. These acquisitions were the beginning of substantial Japanese investments in Hawai'i.

In the early postwar years, the yen-to-dollar exchange rate had created an opposite effect. The official rate in those days was 360 yen to one dollar, with the market rate being closer to 400 yen to one dollar. Because Japan was just recovering economically from the devastation of World War II, its economy was weak. The Japanese had the reputation of being copycats who produced shoddy, imitation goods. The trade imbalance was heavily in favor of the United States. With this dollar shortage, only Japanese businesspeople doing business with Americans were permitted to travel to the United States and then only under tight governmental currency restrictions. The Japanese government allowed them to legally convert yen for only about 1,500 U.S. dollars on their business trips. With these exchange constraints, which were clearly too restricting, I was frequently asked by my Japanese business friends to provide additional U.S. dollars to supplement their dollar allocation by the government. I loaned them the U.S. dollars here and they repaid me in yen when I was in Japan. This helped create the kind of personal relationships that would later keep me in good stead in Japan.

As my friendships and informal business arrangements with these Japanese businessmen grew, I was asked to represent their interests in Hawai'i and the United States through my law practice. One of my earliest associations with a large Japanese corporation was through a local friend in the late 1960s. A Japanese retail company was negotiating with a U.S. company to purchase an old line of retail stores in Honolulu. The local contact suggested that they discuss the matter with me. One night at home I received a long-distance call from Japan. A bilingual executive of the company explained to me in flawless English that his boss was in New York City at that very moment talking with the executives of the U.S. company for the purchase of the Honolulu retail stores. He asked if I would be available to go to New York immediately for about three or four days to help negotiate and, if possible, close the deal. His boss had to leave, but he would fly to New York to meet me and help in the negotiations. He would serve as the contact person with the home office in Tokyo.

I was not particularly interested in the proposal. There was no way I could drop everything to travel to New York City. He talked to me for over an hour, trying to persuade me to represent them. Finally, I agreed to go to New York on the condition that I could travel over the weekend to meet him. He could then bring me up to date on the status of the negotiations and define the economic parameters necessary to close the deal. I could only stay two working days since I had commitments at home. He understood. Over the weekend, I flew to New York City. We established broad parameters on the price and other purchase terms and the various options we could put on the table. Any changes beyond the parameters were subject to his firm's consent. Within two days we were able to successfully close the negotiations to acquire the Hawai'i retail stores.

The more I got involved with these types of business transactions, the more I traveled to Japan and the more I saw the complex interaction of economic forces in an international setting. I stressed to my friends in Japan that when they came to Hawai'i, they had to realize that the laws and rules were different. Business practices were not necessarily the same. Similarly, if they went to the mainland United States, the rules might be even more different. Their evaluation of real estate, based on their experiences in Japan, I explained, would not be relevant. Indeed, such assessments could be misleading. When you come to Hawai'i, I warned them, you better not think you can do business like you do in Japan, where business practices and applicable laws differ. Of course, this admonition also holds true for Americans doing business in Japan, as I had learned from the 7-Up experience. When people attempt to set up a business in a foreign land, they need local contacts or friends who can help, plus some working knowledge of how business is conducted there. Otherwise, the odds for failure are great.

My earliest economic dealings with Hong Kong reaffirmed the basic truth that "when in Rome, do as the Romans." Chinn Ho first introduced me to this part of Asia. Although his primary financial dealings were in the United States and Hawai'i, his roots were in China. Recognizing the great potential for growth in this emerging market of the Pacific Rim, one of Chinn's first projects in Asia was the building of a hotel in Hong Kong during the late 1960s. Started and then initially managed by his uncle, in a short time the project got into financial trouble. His uncle lost control of the cost of construction and financing dried up. The Hong Kong Chinese were quite frankly taking him for a proverbial ride. Getting directly involved to save the project, Chinn syndicated additional equity with other investors from Hawai'i to finish the hotel. In the process, I became involved with him in monitoring the construction of the hotel and developing a business plan to operate it.

With the project now assured of completion, we needed to find management to operate the finished hotel. Dean Ho, who was a graduate from the Cornell School of Hotel Management, was involved in the planning and creation of the hotel's business plan. He recommended one of his classmates to become the manager. Together, they provided professional management at the hotel and eventually turned it around into a profitable venture.

During the construction and the early years of the hotel, I traveled to Hong Kong often. At the time, Chinn and some of his overseas Chinese friends opened communication with representatives of the People's Republic of China at the Bank of China, the PRC's major overseas bank in Hong Kong. Chinn was one of the first American businessmen in the Pacific Rim to boldly state that the nations of the region, including the United States, had to do business with the People's Republic of China. He was ahead of his time. To do business with the PRC was still considered politically taboo by the United States. Of course, the Nationalist Chinese government in Taiwan was furious with Chinn for his position toward mainland China. He was not welcomed by the Chinese consulate in Hawai'i.

Since the hotel project was taking place about the same time I was involved with 7-Up in Japan, I knew that if we were going to work out our problems in Hong Kong, we needed to work with someone local whom we could trust and who knew how to do business in that region. There were no fundamental economic differences between Hong Kong and the United States. The Hong Kong dollar was tied to the U.S. dollar. Money is money no matter where you invest, especially in the free Hong Kong market. However, there are structural, cultural, and lan-

guage differences in doing business, plus strong local networking designed to discourage foreign competition in Hong Kong.
Government laws, regulations, and enforcement are sometimes perplexing and biased against outsiders. Networking
among friends is important in doing business in this region,
and operational procedures different from local practices can
be a hindrance rather than an advantage. We learned soon
enough that the daily operations of the hotel required an understanding of the complex Hong Kong systems of food distribution, housekeeping services, labor–management relations,
hotel marketing, and the whole array of daily activities that
needs to be done. The familiar American style of micro management to which we were accustomed could not be easily
transferred to Hong Kong. Differences in these complex systems had to be first recognized so that solutions to the problems could be developed. If an American businessman thinks
that he can forcefully Americanize the Asian system, he has
made his first mistake.

Finding a local trustworthy person to manage is not always
easy. Trusted, local friends are important references in finding
such a person. If friends recommend that person to you and
you employ him or her, the whole cultural spectrum of kin-
ship obligation and shame comes into play, providing you with
your best shield against fraudulent behavior. To find a qualified bicultural managing employee with good credentials, who
understands generally the Western and Eastern styles of doing
business and is sensitive to local tradition and cultural practices, is critically important but difficult. Without such a person, I would not consider doing business anywhere in Asia.
Investments should be made only when the enterprise is managed by someone with sound local knowledge and credentials
who is also taking a risk along with you. Foreign investment in
Asia is exciting with potential for a high return, but it can also
be volatile and extremely risky.

Unfortunately, I still see Americans working in Asia who
show, perhaps unintentionally, mannerisms and attitudes that
downgrade the way business is done locally. The "ugly American" businessman is apparent when he expects business

discussions to be conducted only in English, even though they are negotiating in a non-English-speaking country. Then he insists on doing business just as it is done at home. This attitude shows a "WASPY" disregard for the Asian style of doing business. Without knowing it, Americans can be set up for a fall. They do not seriously try to adjust to the local environment, associating and complaining among themselves in their own private clubs about how backward Asian businesspeople are. When they fail in their endeavors, these Americans get frustrated and start blaming the host society for their failure. This kind of irrational, insensitive attitude toward Asians does not help the American cause.

On the other hand, the successful American businessperson is also alive and well in Asia. These people are flexible and rational and understand that when businesses are willing to change and adjust to the ways of foreign business, the results can be positive and rewarding. No one way is always the right way. A few years ago, the PRC, for example, was attempting to attract foreign investment in Tianjin, an economic zone located at a river port near Beijing. Three multinational American companies, Heinz, Coca-Cola, and Motorola, were interested in setting up business operations there. Two different approaches to doing business were being considered by these companies. Heinz and Coca-Cola joined forces with Chinese partners to do business by way of a joint venture. Motorola decided, with the permission of government authorities, to do business entirely on its own. While they each differed in the way they wanted to operate business in the PRC, all three were examples of enlightened and successful multinational American companies that have developed a history of knowing how to do business overseas.

In the midst of my involvement as a lawyer with all these private Asian ventures, I suddenly assumed my new role as a trustee of the Bishop Estate. As a consequence, my energy and work priorities shifted from doing private ventures to the affairs of the Estate. Except for the pending matters I was committed to complete before assuming my duties as trustee, I stopped representing my Asian friends in my law practice.

During the controversy surrounding my appointment, I was charged with conflict of interest because I represented the Japanese owner of a retail outlet who had subleased from a lessee of the Estate. I warned the company that opponents to my appointment would strike at me for this possible conflict and that the media would jump in to sensationalize this kind of charge. Since the Estate had no direct relationship with this Japanese retail outlet, I advised my clients to ignore the critics. In fact, when I first came to the Bishop Estate, the Estate had virtually no involvement with Asian investors.

One of the most exciting Asian ventures with which I became intimately involved was the Bishop Estate's investment in the Xiamen International Bank. Originally, American Security Bank was asked to be the American component in a joint venture in the Xiamen bank. When First Hawaiian Bank acquired American Security, First Hawaiian did not want to be involved in the Chinese investment. The Estate was asked whether we would be interested in picking up the interest allocated to American Security. My initial reaction was that the proposal seemed too risky. However, after careful analysis of Xiamen's balance sheet, its profit and loss statements, and the current management, the venture seemed like a conservative investment. The fact that the Asian Development Bank and the Long Term Credit Bank of Japan were investing in this bank confirmed our findings. Moreover, this was the first banking joint venture approved by the Central Bank of China and the national government in Beijing. By any measure, this was a safe and sound investment with international significance.

The investment expected from the Estate was relatively small. The Asian Development Bank and Long Term Credit Bank of Japan were investing an amount double ours and we collectively constituted a one-fourth interest in the bank. The bank was at that time already profitable under the management of Eugene Ho, a Western-trained, bilingual chief executive officer. A talented young man who was born in Shanghai and schooled at the University of Chicago, this CEO had extensive banking experience in the Western world, having served for many years with Continental Bank of Chicago in both Chicago and London. When all these factors were added together, the investment in this venture made good sense. In addition, once this relationship was established in China, there was no telling what future opportunities in China would become available to the Estate. Seventy-five percent of the venture was to be owned by various governmental groups within the PRC, including Industry and Commerce Bank of China (ICBC), the largest domestic Chinese bank, a corporation in Fujian Province listed on the Hong Kong stock market, and the Bureau of Construction of Xiamen. Three directors were added to the board of directors (one from each foreign investor) to represent the minority interest of this venture and the remaining seven directors, including the chairman of the board, represented the various Chinese interests of the PRC.

At the bank's board meetings I had the opportunity to get to know my colleagues who represented the various Chinese entities of the PRC, two of whom I had met earlier in Hawai'i. One female board member was a MBA graduate from UCLA. The board met semiannually with the site changing—Xiamen, Hong Kong, Macao, and once in Fuzhou, the capital of Fujian Province. The meetings were scheduled for two days, allowing enough time to conduct business with immediate translation from Chinese into English and English into Chinese. We usually met from 10:00 A.M. to 12:00 P.M., and then after lunch, continued from 2:00 P.M. until 4:00 P.M. The evenings were reserved for dinner in the best Chinese restaurants in town. The next day we followed the same schedule until we finished the board's agenda. Since the board members were experienced and knowledgeable in banking, we had no ideological problems with business matters at the meetings. The agenda usually included banking budgets, operations, interest rate spreads, and other problems involved with the bank business. I never saw any reason to question the board members' attitudes, actions, or motives. They were as interested as we were in establishing a viable and profitable bank.

We once faced a rare problem when the complex political relationship between the interests of the Xiamen bank and the Communist Party hierarchy arose. A business joint venture in Xiamen failed and loans to the joint venture had been guaranteed by various departments of the provincial and national governments. The manager of the bank informed us that the bank loan had not been paid and the guarantees of the governmental departments were not being honored. When the matter was brought to our attention at the board meeting two years later, as the foreign component we indicated our concern. If the guarantees were valid, we explained, then we needed to call them. The bank needed to operate like a bank. If the guarantors failed to honor their commitment, we should sue them to collect on the guarantees. We insisted that we must make every effort to collect what was owed to the bank if we were going to operate as a traditional bank.

Realizing that such actions could embarrass some directors who were closely affiliated to the governmental guarantors, I suggested that we give the manager an additional six months, until the next board meeting, to work out the problem with the guarantors. If there was any problem, I advised the manager to tell the government agencies involved that "those foreigners" on the board of directors insisted that he collect on the guarantees. To a few board members, calling the guarantees was like asking their political bosses to pay. One Chinese board member agreed with us that it would be appropriate to collect and the guarantors should honor their commitment.

Six months later the problem was still not resolved. The bank was being stonewalled by guarantors of the failed venture. As instructed by the board, the manager of the bank had sued the guarantors of the failed venture. I was informed that the governor of the province then called the bank manager and asked him to withdraw the suit. The bank manager was called to attend the Communist Party meeting, where he was labeled the worst Party member in Xiamen. When the dust finally settled, however, an arrangement was made for the guarantors to pay the bank what was owed it.

Old practices are changing. With foreign joint ventures government interference is minimized. Accounting is straightforward and honest. One reason that Chinese businessmen in

PRC are so eager to establish foreign joint ventures is that governmental agencies overseeing their activity can no longer skim company profits. To encourage these foreign joint ventures, the Chinese government is giving tax holidays. Under this system, businesses pay no taxes for two years after they start to make a profit. For the next three years, they pay 50 percent of their taxes. After five profitable years, they pay the regular tax. Foreign investors are given these incentives to bring capital, know-how, and the technologies needed to accelerate the development of the Chinese economy. The PRC now has the problem of an overheated economy and uncontrollable inflation. This has exacerbated the division of the country between the "haves" in the rapidly growing economic zones and the "have-nots" outside in the rural areas. Social unrest is beginning to show. During my last visit to Shenzen, the first thing I noticed was that the driver of our cab sat behind a protective metal net. I was reminded of the cabs in New York City during the 1960s. When I asked my friend about this, he said that the drivers were protecting themselves from being robbed. Young people from the poor neighboring farm districts were moving into the cities looking for work and had turned to petty thievery since no jobs were available. In the shopping section of Shanghai you can see both the well-dressed affluent Shanghainese and the dirty impoverished farmers who came in from outlying districts. More than political ideologies or human rights, this dichotomy between affluence and poverty is the seed of possible social upheaval in this vibrant but unequal society.

Despite these problems, China's growth is inevitable. The nation has substantial natural resources, an educated populace, and a huge potential market. In addition, labor costs in China are low and economic reform is moving the country toward a market economy. With domestic and foreign investment, the economic development in the coastal regions has exploded. China's economy is continuing to grow as other changes are being made to encourage further development. Currency is being stabilized for monetary exchange in the global marketplace. The official Chinese exchange rate has been replaced by the market exchange rate for commercial transactions. Other commercial practices are being adjusted to conform to global trade requirements.

While China is moving economically toward a commercial marketplace economy, the political apparatus of the communist government is still being maintained. This may seem like a contradiction in terms, but China marches to its own drumbeat in distinguishing between commercial and political activities. The political volatility and unrest seemed exacerbated when I was there by the questions of succession in the Party leadership after Deng Xiaoping and the anticipated problems relating to Hong Kong's transition in 1997. Meanwhile, the Chinese economy will be volatile, with ups and downs in the short run, but growth will occur in the long term.

Unlike many other nations, China will also benefit from the overseas Chinese who have a successful network of wealth and economic power outside China, especially in the Pacific Rim. From Hong Kong to Thailand, Singapore, Malaysia, Indonesia, the Philippines, and Vietnam, many of the leading business leaders, the people with money in these countries, are overseas Chinese with roots in China. Not surprisingly, this group is networked throughout the region. Situated in banking, shipping, real estate, hotel, and other important industrial and technological enterprises, this network is one of the most tightly knit personal-ethnic relationships. The network is made up of individuals with money and business acumen who are bound through family and a common heritage. They are capable of doing business together based on trust or a handshake. Being risk-takers and apolitical, they have real investment opportunities in China. Being familiar with the culture and language, they know how to work with the Chinese bureaucracy by developing their contacts and connections. They will help build the factories and service industries and finance the basic infrastructure improvements for China's roads and bridges. Indeed, the overseas Chinese have provided much of the financial underpinning and know-how of the PRC's economic development in recent years. In addition, they move faster and more decisively than the traditional U.S., Japanese, or European multinational corporation coming into China. For many of these movers and shakers, investing in China is going back to their roots, helping their ancestral nation enter the twenty-first century. This opportunity to help China, plus the opportunity to expand their own economic empire with great potential growth and profit, drives this network of wealthy individuals. When dealing in this region, one has to recognize and appreciate their presence and influence.

The Bishop Estate is also involved in several small joint ventures in China. We have partnered with an experienced entrepreneur, C. B. Sung, who was born, raised, and educated in Shanghai. He emigrated to the United States, receiving an engineering degree from MIT and an MBA from Harvard. Sung worked as a senior executive in a major American industrial company before striking out on his own. Involved as a consultant in a few major PRC joint ventures with American multinational firms, he effectively used his knowledge of China and his connections and peer relationships in these projects. He advised these multinational firms on how to navigate through the cultural and economic intricacies of the Chinese way of doing business. Later, starting his own company, he established a small, domestic niche in business ventures that turned out to be highly profitable. To expand his operations even more rapidly, he sought a financial partner. The Estate became a limited partner in his ventures with established criteria for investments to be made by him in the PRC. Fiscal control by management and a good projected annualized internal rate of return were benchmarks used to determine the value of each investment. The Estate was able to diversify its holdings by investing relatively small amounts in these joint venture projects. We were careful from the start that such investments would not be affected by the Most Favored Nation Treaty of the United States and made sure that international trade politics did not apply. Eventually, our exit strategy was to bring these small but profitable joint ventures together to create a critical economic mass for an initial public offering of stock in Hong Kong or some other public stock market. We would have the option to exit or continue as we thought advisable. While this was going on, our other investment in China, Xiamen International Bank, was considering a public offering to raise additional capital for the bank. The bank planned, with the approval of the Central Bank of PRC, to do a public offering on the Hong Kong market. If and when that occurs, the capital investment of the Estate should increase substantially with ownership of liquid marketable securities of a listed public company in the Hong Kong stock market.

Other economic opportunities are going to open up on various levels throughout Asia in the coming decades. There will be opportunities to invest in financing needed for major infrastructure. This will be through international banking institutions such as the Asian Development Bank, debt financing through American, European, or Japanese investment banking firms, and loans from major American, European, or Japanese banks. At this level the debt structure necessary to build subways, roads, bridges, airports, and other aspects of the infrastructure is huge. The Estate will participate in some of this financing through its interests in Goldman Sachs. On another level, the large multinational companies will enter the Pacific Rim economy with their business know-how, technology, and financial capacity in response to a growing consumer market. Vast investment opportunities will emerge in automobiles, hardware, beverages, and other consumer and industrial products. The market is huge.

One of the most important challenges to the Pacific Rim region in the 1990s is the resolution of economic problems between the United States and Japan. The principal American irritation with Japan is its large bilateral trade deficit, especially in automobiles, auto parts, electronics, and consumer products. As we learned from our 7-Up experience, there are structural impediments to distribution of foreign products in Japan. The hierarchy of the distribution system is inefficient but difficult to challenge. The layers of distribution and networking are controlled through interlocking ownerships of the parties. Under protective laws, even the large Japanese supermarkets such as Seiyu, Daiei, and Ito Yokada need to have the approval of the "mom and pop" stores before moving into the stores' area. The conventional Japanese trading companies, through networking and financial power, control the movement of goods to and from Japan globally, and the very strong middlemen make it extremely difficult for any American business to crack the distribution system and reach the consumer market.

Gradually the system will change. The American firm of Toys 'Я' Us, for example, was finally able to crack the toy market through a joint venture with a Japanese partner in Japan. They have been extremely successful with attractive products at cheaper prices, opening the door to other major American retailers to compete in the high-priced Japanese market. The Japanese retailing system has also been changing. Discounting firms for various products are now challenging traditional retailers. Urban Japanese are buying from these discounters, as consumers are doing in the United States, and the consumer market is reflecting this change.

The kind of American businesses that will break into Asia will be the ones with the economic muscle and good consumer products at reasonable prices. They will persist against the structural roadblocks of Asian law and business practices. Whether the setting is Japan, Taiwan, or Hong Kong, the time and start-up costs of a foreign business will be great. For example, the land costs are high. Land at a good location is often unavailable, unless the American company finds a local partner that already has a location. Toys 'Я' Us adjusted by not locating in Tokyo proper. They opened off a main highway about one hour outside Tokyo. However, since their prices were lower than Japanese prices and they had a greater variety of newer, attractive products that were as good, if not better than, Japanese toys, Japanese consumers came in droves to buy their products. Toys 'Я' Us also engaged in an informative promotional and advertising campaign. Apple Computer and other companies in personal computers also have been able to increase their market share substantially in Japan with quality products at cheaper prices.

Unfortunately, one cannot say the same for the American automobile industry, which complains loudly about the trade imbalance in automobiles and auto parts. While there is validity in the complaint that the Japanese market is not as accessible as the U.S. market (and it will be basically the same for any other Asian market), one wonders how much real effort has been made to market American cars. Laying primary blame on the Japanese government and business practices for their lack of success, these American companies are demanding managed trade by governmental agencies. They ignore the fact that the American automobile may be too large for the streets of Japan, that the steering wheel is placed on the wrong side, or that the quality of the car given the asking price is questionable when compared to a Japanese car. In the free market economy of the United States, the American consumer showed a clear preference for the Japanese car over the American car based on price and quality. Yet American automobile executives are demanding that the Japanese government commit Japanese consumers to purchase American cars. Japanese consumers have the right to make their own choices, just as American consumers do, and they cannot be forced to buy a particular product. No wonder the industry is considered to be made up of "cry babies" and held in such low esteem in Japan. The ultimate result of this kind of tactic by the auto industry is a backlash of anti-American sentiment by Asians such as the Malaysian premier who has charged Americans with arrogance in demanding a share of the market as a matter of right. An Asian regional bloc is developing. Small wonder there is so much anti-American feeling against this attitude of demanding subservience to American interests. We sometimes forget that many Asian nations were under harsh European colonial control only a generation ago, and they are sensitive to, and react bitterly against, any indication of white arrogance.

The truth is that the products from Japan, Taiwan, Korea, Singapore, Malaysia, and Hong Kong have increased their market share in the United States because their quality has been better or the price has been lower. The imbalance in trade exists because American consumers are buying imported products. American companies are not able to compete even in their own market. While you could argue that the inequity is due to the emerging Asian nations' low-wage economy, that is no longer true of a developed nation like Japan, which has some of the highest-paid industrial workers in the world. While some marginal American businesses have clamored for protection, others, especially in the manufacturing sector, have restructured their company to reduce cost, improve quality, and increase productivity to enhance their competitive position globally. The appreciation of the yen, which increases the cost of products made in Japan, has leveled the international monetary field in favor of the United States. But we can expect continual fluctuation caused by volatility of currency exchange, technological improvements, and financial reforms to affect trade in the marketplace. Only time can tell what will happen.

With economic changes and political reforms breaking down the old political power structure, Japanese urban consumers will have far more political clout than rural agricultural interests. Protectionist laws and regulations of marginal business should eventually lessen. In time, urban consumers will demand lower prices, which will give rise to a more efficient commercial system. I sometimes tease my Japanese friends that they pay three times more for rice than I do. And the quality of rice grown in California is as good as any rice grown in Japan. The Japanese must restructure their economy to meet changing times. This restructuring is a direct result of competition in a free market economy, not the result of managed trade quotas between nations.

History shows that oftentimes when American businesses gain a price advantage for their products due to a favorable currency exchange or some kind of governmental assistance, they raise their prices to that of their competitor's to maximize short-term gain instead of keeping their prices low and gaining a greater market share. This phenomenon is a result of the emphasis by the American investment community on short-term instead of long-term return. If they were looking for long-term returns, they would capitalize on this pricing advantage to increase their market share.

The General Agreement on Trade and Tariffs (GATT) is supposed to set a level global playing field for access to various domestic markets. If each business has a level playing field, and if it still cannot compete, then it may not survive without a protective shield. Rather than confront this problem head-on, certain Americans retreat to the notion of "managed bilateral trade." The fallacy is obvious. When economic relations between nations is based on bilateral managed trade, there is no level playing field. Such a condition creates an artificial—if slightly larger—trading market doomed to eventual failure in a global free market economy. This approach is only going to exacerbate trade problems between the United States and Japan in the long run. While the Japanese are likely to accept some form of managed trade for the sake of accommodating the political rhetoric of unfair trade practices, doing so does not resolve the fundamental problem of competition based on price and quality.

Unfortunately, the highly charged political rhetoric over the trade imbalance does not help the situation. Blaming our trading partner for protective barriers or "Japan bashing" is politically popular in the United States. However, the threat of trade sanctions is certainly not the solution to long-range trade problems. This tactic of using threats is changing the political atmosphere in Japan, weakening the political strength of those who want to accommodate the United States and strengthening that of those who follow the dictum of a "Japan who says no." Beset with local political problems and struggling to turn a sluggish domestic economy around, the current ruling majority in Japan is in jeopardy as disenchantment with the United States escalates.

Perhaps American businesses should learn a lesson from the effectiveness of Japanese companies doing business in the United States. These Japanese businesses make extensive feasibility studies before entering the market, research their markets, make long-term financial commitments, and expect losses until they establish themselves. Market share is more important at the outset than profitability. Being patient, they employ local people with extensive training and are quick to adjust to doing business in the local environment.

Some Japanese businesses, however, especially in the acquisition of Hawai'i's luxury hotels in the late 1980s, made the understandable mistake of treating Hawai'i real estate like Japanese real estate. They thought in terms of yen and land prices in Japan. Hawai'i prices seemed reasonable when compared to Japanese prices. However, they were paying a very high price for Hawaiian real estate. They believed that appreciation of real estate values would cover any temporary operating losses incurred in the Hawaiian properties as it did in Japan. Because the first wave of Japanese purchases in Hawai'i was so successful twenty years before, such as Kenji Osano's purchase of ITT's Sheraton, they believed that the trend would repeat itself in the late 1980s. They miscalculated the Hawai'i market. When the Japanese "land bubble" burst, the Hawaiian hotel properties burst as well, with values plunging. In addition, the cost of borrowed money increased substantially. The negative cash flow of the hotels could not be covered with a higher room rate or occupancy, or by appreciation of value in the hotel property. The debt could not be serviced, and eventually the debt exceeded the value of the collateral. With lower revenues than anticipated, high debt service, rising cost of doing business, and plunging real estate values, the end was inevitable. The lenders foreclosed, the properties were gone, and the lenders had problem loans in their banking portfolio. This painful and wrenching process is still going on in the late 1990s. The Japanese investors made the classic mistake of miscalculating in a different business environment. They are now paying a high price for their mistake.

The Japanese use of an advantageous yen-to-dollar exchange rate, which allowed them to enter the U.S. economy with such force, caused some criticism in our community. Japanese Americans were again caught in the middle of this crisis. They could use their unique role to help ease some of these tensions. I sometimes wonder whether future generations will be able to

cope with cultural clashes as readily as the nisei. Educated totally in American schools, speaking only English, and raised
primarily with Western values and attitudes, the third- and
fourth generations may be ill-prepared to play an effective me-
diating role. Although the young generations are ethnically
Asian, their Asian culture and mores seem to have considerably diminished. To appreciate and perhaps retain their cultural heritage, Hawaiʻi's youth must be given tangible and
meaningful opportunities to study and learn Asian languages
and culture. Our educational system should have a second language requirement like the European and Asian educational
systems. By the time many third -and fourth-generation Asian
Americans recognize the value of knowing the language and
cultural heritage of their ancestors, it may be too late.

    Of course, just being ethnically Japanese does not automat-
ically open doors in Japan. Japanese Americans may not be
aware of how Westernized they have become until they meet
their Japanese counterparts in Japan. Western education and
cultural influences are accentuated when you meet someone
who is physically similar to you but raised and educated in a
totally different environment. It is understandable that Japanese nationals do not feel comfortable dealing with nisei
whose language skill is generally poor and inadequate. While
similarity based on physical characteristics creates a certain
sensitivity, culture and environment magnify differences. I
can be comfortably anonymous in Japan because I look like
other Japanese in a crowd, while I feel somewhat uneasy in
the streets of any U.S. metropolis because I look different
from most others. Yet I can more easily relate to lifestyles in
the United States than to those in Japan because of my language and education. This ironic difference in my comfort
level constantly reminds me that I am predominately Western, but Asian in orientation and perception. This unique position struck me when I was asked by a prominent Japanese
friend to entertain privately a member of the Japanese Imperial family and his wife who were visiting Hawaiʻi. We dined
privately at an elegant French restaurant in Waikiki with a
few of my island friends. Knowing his lineage, I wanted him

to know who and what we were—the children of Japanese immigrants born in Hawai'i. My father left Japan, I told him, because he was poor and burdened with debt. My mother was a "picture bride." I was second generation, a member of the 442nd Infantry Regiment, commonly referred to as *nisei butai* with an unequaled record of valor and honor in the American military. Now I was the attorney for his friend in Japan who had asked that I entertain him and his wife privately. In Japan, I said, for someone like me to entertain a royal personage as casually as we were doing that evening in Hawai'i would have been unthinkable. Instead of being offended by my remarks, he said that he understood. Later in Japan, when I met our mutual friend, he called and tried to reciprocate for my hospitality in Hawai'i. Our schedules, however, conflicted and we were unable to do so. Eventually, we lost touch with each other.

To be Caucasian in Japan may sometimes be an advantage. Since Caucasians look different physically from the Japanese, they are not expected to act and be "Japanese" in the same way as nisei. Any attempt by Caucasians to learn the language or acquire cultural knowledge of Japan can be a huge plus. No such credit is given to the nisei, who are somehow expected to have such knowledge and skills. In spite of the difference in expectations, many Japanese businesspersons have confided in me that if Japanese Americans can patiently develop the much needed personal relationships and acquire a working knowledge of the language, Japanese nationals would feel more comfortable with them than Caucasians, because of a common appearance and heritage. There is sometimes a very delicate, unspoken balance in these cross-cultural situations. When the gender issue is added to the equation, the situation becomes even more complex.

Over the years, I am relatively certain that my Japanese friends and I have established long and lasting friendships. Our differences are recognized, but they serve as the bond of understanding for each other. I believe my friends in Japan now see me for what I am. The key to developing that respect is showing them that, as in any long-term relationship, you appreciate and reciprocate their trust and friendship. In the past

decade, my involvement in a small cable television venture involving Japan has helped enhance the cultural bonds with my
ancestry. Nippon Golden Network (NGN), a cable television
channel featuring Japanese programming with English subti-
tles, grew out of an idea of a University of Hawai'i professor,
Dr. Dennis M. Ogawa. Dr. Ogawa wanted to televise Japanese
programs, movies, and daily NHK news to the issei and older
nisei at prime time. This cable channel would fill the void
caused by the cancellation of prime time Japanese TV programs in Honolulu. Capital was raised in Japan and Hawai'i to
begin this venture. Although the project was risky, the need to
provide this service for the non-English-speaking issei was
real. NGN succeeded, and a decade later expanded to offer Japanese programming to visitors from Japan. It also added direct
satellite programs, particularly *sumo*, from Japan to Hawai'i.
As the idea became a reality, credit for this success should go
primarily to Dr. Ogawa and the staff at NGN. My small involvement in this success gives me a personal sense of satis-
faction in filling this need of the issei and nisei, a segment of
the community with which I have a special attachment.

When I deal with people of any background, I cannot forget
my simple, humble, and poor roots as a child in Waialua. I
want people to know that I am not putting them on—that I
am simple, candid, honest, and believe what I am saying. Still,
there are adaptations that I have learned when dealing with
individuals from the East and West. In the case of my Japanese
friends and clients, if I do not agree with them to some degree,
I try to be more considerate and sensitive to their feelings
than I would be with an Occidental. I will patiently try to explain our differences and understand their rationale, minimiz-
ing their "loss of face." However, if openly telling them the
truth becomes important, then I will tell it directly, prefaced
with apologetic language, drawing back when I see them become uncomfortable. Of course, I have learned that this kind
of frankness is never done publicly—only in private, so that
no one is embarrassed.

This is why it is so important to socialize with Japanese
clients. In fact, such interactions are as important in doing

business as formal meetings. It is during the social interactions that you feel *hara,* translated as "what's in the stomach," or what is the true feeling of both parties. Character and attitude, which can affect business relations, sometimes show more clearly when people are playing golf. How they engage in play may reflect how they will act in business. Socializing in a bar allows a similar opportunity to observe or evaluate how well you would be able to get along with a new business associate. Drinking brings out sincerity and openness as inhibitions are loosened and real feelings surface. After you have engaged in the process of meeting, going to dinner, and going to a bar with a Japanese business client again and again over a period of a few years, a good personal relationship can be formed. Only then will the discussions get more informal and honest. Yet no matter how uninhibited you may be at these moments, losing your sensitivity is a cultural taboo.

Today, I consider myself extremely fortunate to have experienced all that I did in Japan, the PRC, and other Pacific Rim nations. These experiences taught me the role Hawai'i can play in the Pacific Rim and how the islands can contribute and enhance social understanding and economic growth in the region. As my involvement in Asia, particularly Japan, continues, I like to believe that I have contributed in a small way to the promotion of goodwill and understanding of the peoples in these areas. By maintaining my affiliation with the NGN cable television channel, I can continue to play a small role in the cultural interaction of Japan and Hawai'i. As the new century approaches, I believe Hawai'i, located at the midpoint between the continents of North and South America and Asia, will be in a pivotal position to bring mutual understanding and cultural sensitivity to the entire Pacific Rim. As I count my blessings of the past, I look to a future where strides can be made for Hawai'i to truly fulfill at last its potential as the Crossroads of the Pacific.

CHAPTER SEVEN

Reflections from inside Hawai'i

THE HAWAIIAN ISLANDS have experienced many changes in the past fifty years that have revolutionized our society, economy, and way of life. In retrospect, the bombing of Pearl Harbor, the advent of World War II, the triumphs of the 100th Battalion and 442nd and the military intelligence groups, and the political and economic changes of the 1950s seem like fortuitous events, giving rise to opportunities to be grasped and creating milestones on the path to a freer and more democratic island society. In the nisei's effort to modernize Hawai'i, it would be presumptuous and untrue to assume that our generation achieved these changes without assistance from our friends of all races who shared similar hopes and aspirations. Whether we were Hawaiian, Japanese, Chinese, Filipino, Okinawan, or Korean, we all carried within us basic values of family pride, commitment, and obligation.

From my Japanese side I inherited certain values that have stayed with me throughout my entire life—my sense of loyalty, devotion to family and friends, and the need to fulfill my obligations. These basic values transcend race and wealth, and serve as the foundation for long-term trust and friendship among Hawai'i's people. Between friends who share these values, words are unnecessary. You always are assured that if you look over your shoulder, your friends are right there behind you.

These values serve as guideposts for personal ethical behavior and for evaluating others. As relationships develop over the years with a great variety of friends and business partners, certain characteristic behavior evolves, which becomes pre-dictable. "Our lives are connected," an old Japanese adage says, "with the brush of our kimono sleeves." This attitude of reciprocal relations is standard operating procedure, almost in-stinctive at times, and becomes increasingly important as one's ability to affect the lives of others becomes greater. Indi-vidual decision-makers who have reached the highest levels of economic influence and prestige care more about meaningful, trusting friendships than the symbols of status. The truly suc-cessful individual is an unassuming person who never forgets the courtesy and respect due to others.

A product of multicultural Hawai'i, the interplay of West-ern, Asian, and Polynesian cultures has shaped my ability to appreciate and juggle various settings from New York City and Washington, D.C., to Tokyo and Beijing. I have often been able to facilitate the mutual understanding required during meet-ings between Asian and American businesspeople. One of the most important contributions Hawai'i can make to the future of the Pacific Rim is the continued enhancement of this aware-ness of, and appreciation for, cultural pluralism. The islands have long been recognized as an appropriate place to integrate Asian and Western perspectives for the benefit of the global economy. For those of us with this unique multicultural up-bringing, serving as a personal bridge between these various worlds can be an exciting opportunity, as the future "super-highway" of communication shapes the next century.

Although some critics have lamented the substantial influ-ence tourism has on the island economy, particularly Japanese tourism, the visitor industry will continue to play a major economic role in Hawai'i's future into the twenty-first cen-tury. The importance of Japanese tourism for the islands was evident during the Gulf War and resulting recession in Japan, when the visitor count dropped drastically. This had a ripple effect on all levels of Hawai'i's economy. However, Hawai'i's future as a resort destination for the Japanese cannot be taken for granted. While the islands' incomparable location in the middle of the Pacific, its beautiful weather, luxury accommo-dations and amenities, multicultural people, and warm Polynesian culture are attractive advantages, other destinations, like Hong Kong, Australia, and Guam, are vigorously competing for the same Japanese tourist dollars. These markets have aggressively sought Japanese tourists with attractive packages of air travel and accommodations at lower prices, promises of different experiences, and a greater effort to show hospitality and service.

However, as long as Hawai'i is high on the list of special destinations, continues to be affordable to visitors, and puts out a warm and *real* welcome mat, we will get our share of new and repeat visitors. With Korea, Taiwan, and emerging Pacific Rim nations growing economically, people in these countries are beginning to have discretionary dollars to spend, and they will also come to Hawai'i. In a multicultural society with so many island people having Asian roots, these new visitors can feel comfortable and accepted.

Japan today still provides the most visitors from the Pacific area, even though the profile of the Japanese tourist to Hawai'i has changed over time. Instead of the large tour groups of the past, the islands will see more repeat visitors, "office ladies" (young working women) and "silver ladies" (older matured married women) who will travel independently. Young travelers buy more windbreakers and sweatshirts with printed decals than high-end designer handbags and dresses. The neighbor islands, instead of Waikiki, will become an alternative experience for many of these repeat visitors, who will seek a different feel and perspective. Hawai'i today is not a one-dimension destination area. We can arrange a wide array of experiences for the tourist, from Waikiki to Maui, Hawai'i, Kauai, and Lanai. Hopefully, we will be able to adjust, meeting the various expectations of visitors from both East and West. The Convention Center will add another dimension to our visitor industry by attracting conferences of sizable business, professional, and fraternal organizations. With creative responses to an ever-changing market, Hawai'i must continue to be a major resort area attracting the widest range of visitors to our shores. Tourism today remains our most important industry with the greatest growth potential in the future.

The only cautionary note is whether the sometimes volatile Hawaiian sovereignty movement will erupt as an anti-tourist movement affecting the service or safety of our visitor friends. While cyclical economic conditions cause ups and downs in a discretionary dollar industry such as tourism, reputation for lack of safety, poor service, and an "unwelcome" mat would permanently affect the visitor industry. We need to constantly remind ourselves that we cannot take our visitors for granted.

While the opportunity to develop other industries in Hawai'i such as high technology should be explored, realistically the potential is limited. The islands do not have leading research-oriented universities like Silicon Valley in California, Raleigh-Durham Research Center in North Carolina, or Route 120 near Boston. The University of Hawai'i does not have the educational and research stature to meet that need. While a lower-level technology center may be possible, distribution to the ultimate user located far away from Hawai'i will continue to be a serious problem. Hawai'i is in the middle of the Pacific Ocean, thousands of miles away from the continental United States or Asia. Our foreign trade center in Hawai'i demonstrates this weakness because we are simply too far away from the major markets of the continental United States. Multinational businesses and industries will locate themselves closer to the main marketplaces. Consequently, no matter how one analyzes our economic possibilities, the real viable growth industry will continue to be the visitor industry.

As far as Hawai'i's sugar industry is concerned, like the dinosaurs who became extinct, our sugar plantations are failing one at a time. The announcement of the closing of Waialua Sugar Plantation is hitting pretty close to home since I was born and raised in Haleiwa. I worked on this sugar plantation. Waialua was my childhood home where I earned my first dollar. My brother and his family still live there, along with many of my classmates from Waialua High School. Since the lands of the plantation are partially owned by the Bishop Estate, I knew that it was only a question of "when" and not "if" the plantation would shut down. With low sugar prices on the international market and the federal subsidy inadequate to meet the high costs of operation, the plantation could not survive. Losing millions of dollars each year as a private company, the plantation became an economic casualty. Other sugar plantations may follow unless they become more efficient and procure enough subsidy to be profitable. The future, however, looks bleak. The demise of sugar, as we knew it in the past, seems inevitable. The low cost of "coolie" labor supplied by our immigrant parents is gone. The sugar industry cannot compete in the current international market without major government support.

As the plantations close, vast acreage will become available for alternative use. The utilization of these lands in a way that will provide jobs, income, and profit, as the sugar plantation did in the past, is going to be a serious land use issue on all the islands. At Waialua and the Hamakua coast of Hawai'i, finding new viable land uses will challenge the best minds of business and government. Oahu Sugar will have less of a problem since it is near urban Honolulu, where industrial, commercial, and residential development is possible. Guava, coffee, and diversified agriculture, including flowers, avocados, and papayas, can be developed on a smaller scale, but the emergence of a major agricultural use comparable to sugar and pineapple is not realistically on the horizon. The situation poses a difficult land use problem and only close, coordinated cooperation between government and private industry can minimize the impact of the demise of this agricultural industry.

A truly vital concern involving the economic future of Hawai'i is the lack of opportunities for talented young people. Highly trained and professionally educated, they do not have job opportunities in Hawai'i that they can find on the mainland. After graduation from first-rate universities away from Hawai'i, many do not return home. As I think ahead, I am concerned about my grandchildren's future in Hawai'i. Will they find the kind of professional opportunities open to them in Hawai'i when they finish their college education? My parents' generation could realistically look beyond laboring in the sugar plantation community for their children who could go to college and become teachers. The second generation became involved in a war and came back from the battlefields of Europe and Asia with an opportunity to pursue higher education using the GI Bill. Our children inherited the fruits of their nisei parents' efforts, getting more education and stepping up the economic ladder as wage earners, businesspeople, and professionals in a relatively free and open environment. Now, however, in a matured society, when my grandchildren graduate from high school, university, and perhaps graduate school, will Hawai'i be able to provide them with opportunities that match their abilities and professional skills in a high-tech, computer-driven world?

The reason for Hawai'i's lack of economic choices is in part due to the minimal opportunities for small businesses. The islands are blessed with good year-round weather, an ambiance as good as any in the world, and a wonderful environment in which to live. However, Hawai'i is an island state with a cost of living higher than most parts of the mainland. This high cost of living, together with high taxes and a burdensome regulatory climate, make doing business costly and difficult. The result is that many local residents move to places like Nevada, particularly Las Vegas, where they pay no state income tax and the cost of living is lower. A house in Nevada costs substantially less than one in Hawai'i. The costs of food, clothing, and shelter are much lower and job opportunities in the area are greater. Silicon Valley in California has also attracted some of our most talented young people. Opportunities for them to use their highly trained skills are available with major business enterprises.

One of the economic changes that has taken place in the past forty years is the diminished opportunity of the small entrepreneur to participate in the growth of the islands. During the 1950s, there was a minimal planning and zoning process and less government regulation, allowing small building contractors to develop residential land. Today, many of these entrepreneurs have disappeared. They cannot compete in the regulatory maze of land use and zoning, which requires time, money, and staying power to survive. The process is complex and causes delay. Small building contractors today are limited to the construction or remodeling of homes for one client at a time; they are no longer involved in the risk-taking venture of building and selling a house and lot to the ultimate buyer. Today, land use and zoning laws require one to go through a state and county planning process that calls for political connections and takes years to complete, demanding substantial front-end capital and financial resources. Without the deep pocket to carry the costs during this approval process, a developer cannot survive. Only after the governmental process is completed through bureaucratic commissions and political councils can the infrastructure be initiated and installed and the first nail pounded into the house. Consequently, the development field is closed except to the biggest players with available capital and financial resources. Small contractors have almost completely vanished.

There is no question that houses have to be built at affordable prices to meet the continuing need of our people. But the government's requirement that developers provide affordable housing at prices below market cost is another constraining economic factor. The costs incurred by the developers complying with this government requirement are shifted to other homes priced at whatever the market can bear. This creates a peculiar housing market environment. Homeowners who qualify for below-market affordable housing get a windfall while prices for everyone else skyrocket. The government requirement for affordable housing is not good market practice. Only limited numbers of developers can afford to comply with this requirement, which further discourages competition in the housing market.

While government subsidies are needed to meet the social needs of the poor and needy, the use of government power to demand that the private sector favor one group over another seems unreasonable and unwise. Such practices lead to more bureaucratic regulation instead of less government interference. If an affordable housing requirement is deemed necessary, then legislation to build such homes should be established to apply to everyone equally. That way, individual land use applications could be processed immediately so long as developers can show compliance with the legislation. There should be a conscious effort to promote competition among builders and developers by making land readily available for housing development. Well-located, unused sugar lands should be made available for housing. In this way, the marketplace could encourage a more than adequate supply of housing to meet the various needs of society. A free competitive market will put a lid on prices, and supply may quickly meet the demand for housing. Of course, this rational free market solution will probably not happen since the prospects for reducing or eliminating political and regulatory control and planning by government is unlikely. Sometimes I think Houston, Texas, has the solution to our housing crisis. There are no zoning requirements in Houston; the market determines the use.

As it stands now, government has discretionary power to approve or deny private plans for land use. Public hearings need to be held. Public input adds to the complexity and confusion. The bureaucracy micro-manages development as part of the planning approval process. The government also attempts to respond to various proposals of community and political groups that attempt to change and revise the plans. All of this adds substantial cost and delay to the final product.

I can accept the concept of macro planning by government to achieve a societal goal. Government should set broad, understandable guidelines applicable to everyone. Beyond setting certain parameters for safety and land use, such as infrastructure requirements, building codes, and environmental standards, however, government should limit its interference with development in the marketplace. The private sector is better able to meet and understand the needs of the community. To survive, it must be rational and build what is marketable to the public. Big government should not be the solution to social and economic needs, but the facilitator of development of ways to meet community needs. Very limited discretionary power should be given to government bureaucrats to apply these standards. Less, not more, government regulations are needed to make meaningful progress.

For Hawai'i, as the Bishop Estate has become reputedly "big and powerful," greater media attention has been inevitable. However, the media has chosen its turf very carefully in the targeting of the Estate. While the press often commends the educational legacy of Princess Pauahi's will, they are also highly critical of the commissions paid to the trustees. However, when the press harshly criticizes the trustees for taking a strong position on behalf of the Estate against residential lessees acquiring a fee interest from the Estate, they ignore the fiduciary duty of the trustees to preserve and protect the assets of the Estate. The trustees in these instances are pictured as "greedy and unreasonable" lessors fighting for the best possible value of assets they were forced to sell by law. Such reporting is blatantly inconsistent, unbalanced, and a contradiction in terms. The media coverage of the trustees of the Bishop Estate either condemns them or ignores their basic fiduciary responsibilities, as they deem convenient. Rarely are the trustees ever credited with possessing any intelligence or business acumen.

A review of the newspaper coverage of the activities of the Bishop Estate over the past decade reveals a continuous, one-sided litany of attacks. Articles criticize the trustee appointment process established by the testatrix; they sensationalize problem areas in the Estate's portfolio of investments, usually emphasizing the allegations of the people who caused the problem in these investments. The reporters who do the investigative reporting often have little working knowledge of investment banking, private placement investments, or the tax code, as it applies to these investments. In many cases they are looking to sensationalize the problem workouts by trying to uncover conflicts of interest to attack the veracity of the trustees. In each one of these cases, the newspaper article fails to explain that mismanagement of the project by others, and in one case, outright fraud by the managing general partner, not the trustees, caused the problem. This particular problem required the Estate to change from passive investor to active manager of the investment project. This changed the tax status of the investment from generating tax-exempt income. The Estate had to assign its passive limited partnership interest to a stock interest in its taxable subsidiary in order to replace the incompetent or crooked management. While the press suggested there was something "sinister" about these actions, the Estate clearly proceeded within the purview of the tax code, protecting its tax-exempt status by having its taxable subsidiary conduct the active workout of unrelated business activities.

Uninformed reporters trying to pin conflict of interest on the trustees also fail to understand a basic tenet of making an investment: all parties involved must be at risk. Everyone must "put his money where his mouth is." If decision-makers make personal investments parallel to the entity for which the decision is being made, they reaffirm their judgment in the investment. Instead of conflict, it is a vote of confidence concerning the investment decision. Stock options for executives of a public company show this same parallel economic interest of executives and their company. While the press portrays these private investments as somehow questionable, the world of business encourages risk–reward to executives for performance and investment risk-taking with their company. Reporters, however, pay little heed to this risk incentive factor in business practices, trying to read into this situation "avarice," "conflict," and "insider information" to imply misconduct. They rarely take any risks in either the business world or the political world.

I have sometimes been the target of biased media reporting. In one instance the newspaper ran a front-page banner headline with my picture, declaring that "Takabuki was in conflict of interest." Written by a reporter who was perhaps seeking recognition, the whole story was predicated on an outright lie. I complained to the "independent" media council as well as the editors of the paper. The chairman of the council, who was also employed by the newspaper company, hedged his response, trying to rationalize the reporter's obvious error and bias on his inability to interview me. The editors a week later published a very equivocating retraction, which occupied two inches in an unobtrusive corner of the front page. Journalistic integrity seems like meaningless rhetoric.

From this experience I quickly learned that the so-called independent council set up to hear complaints against media was basically a facade and shield for the media. Except for a few reporters I know personally, I generally have a very low opinion of journalists. As one of my friends once reassured me, if the press is predisposed to do a "hatchet job" on you, anything you say will be of no avail. To be fair and balanced in reporting is not part of their makeup since newspapers sell sensational stories. As a consequence, I have learned to ignore the media, knowing that whatever they say has little significance with a short shelf life.

The public's perception of the Kamehameha Schools/ Bishop Estate is ambivalent, perhaps because of media coverage. On the one hand, many people agree that KSBE provides a good school for Hawaiian children. On the other hand, others view the KSBE as a private trust worth billions, with large landholdings and other financial assets, which uses its financial and political muscle to the detriment of the general public. The trustees, who are appointed by justices of the Supreme Court to run the affairs of the trust, receive allegedly astronomical compensation. This issue is a favorite target of the press. They are critical of the appointive process by the Supreme Court to name successor trustees because matters involving the Estate may come before the Court. However, the press does not suggest an alternative appointive body, but simply sees the appointive choices as being "political." Given the press's tacit approval of the appointment of white business executives to other estates, the bias of the press against appointees of color to the Bishop Estate raises "political" questions as to their underlying bias. This criticism did not occur when white business executives were appointed to run the affairs of the Estate, a situation that existed for decades before the political and judicial changeover from white Republican to local non-white Democratic control of the government. I sometimes wonder how today's press would treat the Estate if it were as white-dominated as the other trust. Would they then drop the "political hack" or "unqualified" charges that are currently used against the present part-Hawaiian trustees? Would the public criticisms about the commissions paid to the trustees be generally muted as they are for commissions paid on a higher percentage to another comparable trust under state law?

Whatever their motive, the press continues to single out the Estate, depicting it as a large, greedy landowner exploiting the small, weak lessee on their land. News articles fail to indicate that legislation in this field has been heavily tilted toward the lessees. Numbers, and sympathetic arguments fanned by the press, helped lessees against lessors in the political arena. News coverage failed to indicate the huge windfall in value the lessees enjoyed in the forced leasehold conversion law. It is this anomaly in compensation that left landowners with such a bitter aftertaste and has led to continual challenges to any leasehold conversion legislation at every step. Fairness seems to dictate a more balanced treatment of the equities of the lessor and lessee in this controversy. But such was not the case in media reporting. The landowners could only tell their side of the story through paid advertisements in the press and on television.

Other activities of the Estate have faced the same unfair reporting by the media. Journalistic liberties were sometimes taken in interpretive reporting based on wild allegations and half truths made by adversaries of the Estate. Troubled projects were emphasized while successes were ignored. Instances have actually occurred where business journalists made charges without knowing the very issue they were covering. They did not understand basic financial terms like "puts" and "calls," and how they were used to hedge investments. With the news media accentuating the negative, it is no wonder Goldman Sachs, like the Estate, avoids print and electronic media.

The favorite media coverage of the Estate is the annual commissions trustees receive. Each time this issue is raised, the specific amount is emphasized, implying that the commission is excessive. Rarely will the report state that the trustees' fees are based on a fixed percentage of qualified income receipts established by state law for charitable institutions. While the voluntary waiver of substantial amounts of fees is mentioned, the media suggests that such waivers are not enough. Rarely does the news coverage compare the percentage of income allocable as compensation to trustees of private trusts, which is 5 percent, to the 2 percent allocable for a charitable trust. Several decades ago, a Bishop Estate trustee resigned to take an appointment with another trust because of the differential in compensation. Legislation can change this commission schedule. Many years ago the legislature in fact reduced the percentage from 5 percent to 2 percent for charitable trusts. The Estate was clearly the target of this law. Only recently, when the Estate's receipts increased more than tenfold, did the media begin to focus on statutory fees of the trustees. In doing so, the coverage emphasized only the amount received. It neglected to say that the commission schedule did not change; the increase was due solely to greatly increased revenues of the Estate. The compensation amount was calculated after a substantial voluntary waiver of compensation. I cannot imagine how any beneficiary of the institute would want the Estate to have less revenues in order to avoid paying trustees a compensation based on 2 percent of revenues. The media's rationalization seems to be that since the Estate is a charity, the trustees should accept less.

The Estate is seldom given credit by the media as a sophisticated investor comparable to other major eleemosynary institutions like Harvard, Duke, or the McArthur Foundation. As one legendary investor once said to me, "The Estate must be doing something right. Your name is often mentioned on the Street. And I know you are sought after by the real big players on Wall Street like Goldman Sachs and J. P. Morgan." The local media never credits the Estate in the same positive light as these highly regarded professionals. One would think that, perhaps, people in general would actually be proud that a local group has been able to achieve a highly respected status as a knowledgeable and prudent investor on Wall Street.

Indeed, if one were to believe the local media coverage and television reports like CNN's "Moneyline," one would conclude that the Bishop Estate is an evil, greedy institution that practices racial and religious discrimination. Charges are made that the Estate exploits the small, weak residential lessees; it is a political powerhouse, influencing legislators to do its bidding; it violates the Civil Rights Act by admitting only part-Hawaiian children to Kamehameha Schools; it practices religious discrimination in hiring only Protestant teachers; it is generally a disreputable Hawaiian institution in a tourist Mecca called Hawaiʻi. This kind of news reporting fails to give credit to the Hawaiian princess who left her entire estate to provide the means to educate her disadvantaged people. Maybe media should listen to the students of Kamehameha Schools in order to appreciate the impact of this legacy of hope for this disadvantaged group through education. If the individuals who are benefited by the Estate are interviewed and quoted, maybe something positive can balance the distorted picture of the Estate portrayed by the media. However, the mainland, white-controlled press, who cares less about the history of the local multicultural racial heritage of Hawaiʻi, cannot perceive or value the character of historical changes in our uniquely constructed society.

Such criticisms also obscure the truth that only a few non-white companies like the Bishop Estate are making their mark in the national and international capital market and fails to question the wrong local impression that non-whites cannot effectively compete in the global investment arena. At the highest levels of Hawaiʻi's private corporations, many young educated islanders sense that they face a "glass ceiling" in upward mobility. While the color line has blurred considerably, opportunities in white corporate culture may still not be as available as they should be. Just as for African Americans, it is rare for a local non-white to be a top corporate executive in the white business world. When the appointed judiciary was predominantly white, chosen by a white governor who was in turn chosen by the White House, the trustees were predominantly white with *kamaaina* Merchant Street ties. In those days the media did not criticize the Estate. While the appointive process remains the same, the vast political and racial changes of the past four decades have drastically transformed the racial makeup of the trustees. It has gone from a predominantly white club to the present board of part-Hawaiians. Recently arrived whites who control the media and some public interest groups now criticize the appointive process and attack current appointees as "political" or "unqualified." The media seems to hint that a truly qualified trustee is a white business executive, like those chosen for another major trust. Even a former governor who happens to be Hawaiian, in their view, would be "political" and "unqualified." Despite their noisy criticisms, the Bishop Estate is now governed by five trustees of Hawaiian ancestry and the days of predominantly white Republican trustees are gone for the foreseeable future. The Estate is a prominent and vivid symbol of the racial diversification of centers of power in Hawai'i. Overall, for Hawai'i and Bishop Estate, these are the concerns and thoughts I held on what the media often reported during my years as a trustee.

All these controversies highlight the often unspoken tensions between local non-whites and whites, particularly recent arrivals who have added a new twist to our traditional race relations. A significant demographic change took place in the 1980s when tens of thousands of out-of-state whites, many military retirees, moved to Hawai'i, some of them bringing to the islands a California-style, confrontational, hard-nosed attitude and rhetoric. This new population added a different dimension to the dynamics of cultural, race, and economic relations in Hawai'i, particularly in the field of politics. The political persuasion of these new residents has ranged from the liberal left of the Rainbow Coalition to the conservative wing of the Christian right. As we watch our highly educated local youth moving to the mainland for greater job opportunities, these new residents seem to have filled the void.

Growing racial tensions surrounding the sovereignty question is an issue the people of the islands will need to address. Symptomatic of this racial unrest is the growing chorus of voices attacking the disproportionate number of nisei teachers and principals in the public school system, charging the DOE with ethnic favoritism or discrimination. What these critics fail to understand is that time and opportunity historically played a part in creating this situation, and time and opportunity in the future will resolve this discrepancy. In the 1950s and 1960s, opportunities for talented and educated local university graduates, especially nisei females, was limited to teaching. Admission of local public high school graduates into Teachers College was very selective. Only those on the academic honor rolls, who were mostly women of Asian ancestry, qualified. Teacher jobs in the public educational system were waiting for these students after graduation from "T.C." Punahou and other private schools, including Kamehameha Schools, primarily selected mainland-trained Caucasian teachers. Public schools at that time reflected the multiethnic student population on the other side of the street. The trained nisei teachers from "T.C." were of the same ethnic mold as the student population.

In time, some of these nisei teachers became principals and then administrators. Those who went on to obtain their graduate degrees also began climbing up the administrative ladder to the top echelon of the school system. Gradually as the more affluent locals sent their children to private schools, the public school population began to change as children of newly arrived immigrant groups became predominant. Today, these children, particularly the young Filipino Americans, are following the path of the nisei a generation ago. They want a piece of the action, and they are achieving greater access to government and business positions. The election of Ben Cayetano, a Filipino American, as governor of Hawai'i is symbolic of this new era.

Despite the interracial tensions that still exist among ethnic groups, and the Hawaiian claim of sovereignty to redress a century-old wrong, Hawai'i is still consciously striving to be the melting pot of the Pacific. The diverse groups and people of Hawai'i struggle for their share of power and influence in all aspects of island life. Our systems are no longer so rigid as to allow only one class or color to control the reins of government. This competitive and fluid situation creates a healthy environment. As long as our people do not expect favored treatment, but only equal opportunity to succeed, our open society will remain democratic, vibrant, and enriching, regardless of race, gender, religion, or creed.

While Hawai'i has many challenges to face in the future, as I reflect on how far we have come in my lifetime, I do not despair. Having traveled the road in one generation from working for a mere pittance in the plantation field, through surviving combat in World War II, serving as an elective politician, having a career as a corporate and real estate lawyer, serving more than twenty-one years as trustee of the largest private education estate, and finally retiring at seventy years of age in 1993, I have lived a full and productive life. In those seventy years, a far more democratic and open society was created. Now there are new problems requiring innovative and creative solutions on the part of present and future generations. While I have concerns about the future, I have enough confidence in my children and grandchildren to know that they will build on the foundations they inherited from us to establish a better future for all people in Hawai'i.

While recently visiting the Japanese American National Museum in Los Angeles, I was moved by a letter prominently displayed in the exhibit "Fighting for Tomorrow." This poignant message from a grandfather to his grandson expresses better than I can the best advice my generation can impart to the future generations:

OCTOBER 7, 1994

Dear Casey Akira:

Grandpa Ohashi is your yesterday. The past. Your Daddy Michael is today. The present. You, Casey, are tomorrow. Or the future.

Whatever we did yesterday and today will affect your future tomorrow. But, you have a rich cultural, traditional, and ethnic heritage. Many young men like you cannot claim the tremendous odds both yesterdays and todays had experienced and overcome.

We still live in a country filled with prejudice and hate. We can't overcome all the ill feelings, suspicions, and insecurity unless all of us are more informed, more tolerant, more educated, and become more respectful of others and learn from our historical strength, weaknesses, errors, and blunders.

Your future won't be easy at all. You'll have a lot more choices and options but selecting the right course of action and making a firm decision with full commitment will not be easy.

In the past, I have learned to work hard, study hard, be honest, be with friends who are successful, and always respect, honor, and obey those people who are more experienced, more knowledgeable, more skillful than you will ever become.

Learn from other people's mistakes. Even those mistakes made yesterday and today are lessons to be learned tomorrow. Honor the country, your parents, and the elders. Be an exemplary citizen in your community and country.

Grandpa and Daddy won't be with you in the future. We only ask that you carry on the family tradition with honor and respect and to the best of your abilities.

Love,

Grandpa James T. Ohashi

As Good as the Next Guy

As I approached mandatory retirement at the age of seventy in 1993, my staff and my daughter began planning a retirement party. Early on, I indicated that I did not want a big celebration at a Waikiki hotel, but a small, informal, by-invitation-only gathering with the Kamehameha Schools' *ohana* and friends. While I was told that the party was going to be in accordance with my wishes, I was not informed of the intended size or scope of the dinner and program. Knowing that I did not want a retirement gift, a scholarship fund in my name was established for Kamehameha Schools.

The invitation list, which I had asked to be kept small, turned out to be a "who's who" of my life. My classmates from Waialua High School were invited, as were my friends from the 442nd. Invitations were sent to friends and colleagues in New York, Washington, D.C., Chicago, Las Vegas, San Diego, Los Angeles, San Francisco, Tokyo, and Hong Kong—many of whom made the effort to travel to Hawai'i just for this event. The luau was held in the schools' largest facility, the Kekukau-pio athletic gymnasium, which had been beautifully decorated by the school cafeteria and support staff. The evening was a wholly unexpected Hawaiian extravaganza.

During the program, Jim Burns and Dean Ho, sons of my old, close, and respected friends, Governor John Burns and Chinn Ho, honored me with speeches. Pinky Thompson, representing the trustees and the Kamehameha *ohana*, offered words of appreciation, while the Association of Hawaiian Civic Clubs awarded me a "Certificate for Excellence as the

1992 outstanding non-Hawaiian for service to the Hawaiian Community." A beautiful *"Mele Inoa No Takabuki"* was also chanted in my honor. Even a special video presentation entitled "Tribute to Takabuki" was prepared by the staff and shown at the dinner. As a final touching tribute, Eric Martinson, Bruce Nakaoka, and Nathan Aipa, talented young men who had worked with me during my years as trustee, quietly presented a white *kukui* nut lei in a small koa bowl. Their gift was a deeply appreciated symbolic Hawaiian gesture of their love, respect, and appreciation for an elder who had taught them important skills and insights to better their lives.

In my parting remarks, I expressed my thanks to all those, past and present, who had touched me in my tenure as trustee. I wanted to leave them a message of *lokahi* or "harmony" as part of my dream, and the dream of Bernice Pauahi Bishop that Kamehameha Schools stand in perpetuity as the institution that helps uplift her people through education. Hopefully, I said, I have met the commitment that I had made more than two decades ago to do the best I could with whatever talent I may have been given. Now that "payoff" time had arrived, I hope I did my job as promised.

Later I would enjoy other retirement parties hosted by my many friends from both sides of the world. In New York City, Jon Corzine, John Twain, and Barry Zubrow of Goldman Sachs honored me with a small party, as did Scott Levine of J. P. Morgan. In Tokyo, my friends of over two decades put together a Japanese-style retirement party. While very different from what happened at the schools, the gathering was very touching for they had made time to honor my *intai* from the Estate. The gifts received at this reception were given to the scholarship fund established in my honor.

During the days after my retirement, people who had once been so vehemently opposed to my appointment twenty-one years earlier were now saying *Mahalo* for what I had done for the Estate. Especially touching was a card inscribed, "There are moments when one person makes a special difference that no one else can make."

While I am a *keiki o ka aina* who earned his place in the sun in Hawaiʻi, I am still a guest of the Hawaiians, the indigenous people of these islands. I sincerely hope that in twenty-one and a half years as trustee of a Hawaiian trust, I paid my debt to them for allowing me to be enriched by these islands. Being hugged and given words of appreciation by my former critics helped ease all the pain and frustration I faced many years earlier. I can now say to anyone, Hawaiian and non-Hawaiian, that my selection as trustee of this Estate was right within the context of that time period. I am proud that I did make a difference to help the Estate become better.

I have learned in my life to live by a simple truth—to use whatever talent I have been given to do the best I can for my family and my community. Having grown up in a Hawaiʻi where poverty and racial restrictions were commonplace, I have been driven by a sense of insecurity and gnawing anger as I sought to achieve my hopes and aspirations. Never forgetting when a quarter was meaningful, I still vividly remember the days when my mother could not give me the spending money I thought I needed to attend a student conference on Maui. She gave me all that she could, and I now realize her sacrifice and love. I never forgot what it meant to be poor. The drive to achieve economic security so that my own children and grandchildren will feel safe and secure in Hawaiʻi has been one of the deepest aspirations shaping my life.

In attaining that economic security, I also wanted to deliver a message to my children and grandchildren—never to question the fact that you're as good as the next guy, no better or no worse, but just as good as you want to be. Whatever you do in your life should depend on your own ability and desire to be successful with hard work. In my life I tried to see that this opportunity would be available not only to my family, but to all the people of Hawaiʻi. This had been the hope and dream of our parents. This was the vision of John A. Burns: to provide everyone in Hawaiʻi with the chance to prove themselves and enjoy the fruits of their labor. This is our simple legacy to those who follow us.

Equity and fairness are valuable tools of life. The fact that a person values these attributes helps him or her deal forthrightly with other people. The most important negotiating principle I followed in every transaction is that all parties in a deal must walk away with the feeling that they were dealt with fairly and that the deal made sense to both parties. If the goal of your negotiations is to outmaneuver or undermine your partners or participants to gain advantage, then that relationship will be short-lived. If you want a long-term relationship that is mutually beneficial, then equity, fairness, and honesty are necessary attributes to bring to the negotiating table. To do less is to violate the very values on which mutual and meaningful partnerships are made.

On the day of my retirement, the bells of Kawaiahao Church rang out in tribute to what I had contributed to the Bishop Estate and the Native Hawaiian community. Many years earlier, those same bells were rung to lament my appointment, an expression of bitterness and anger. This simple tribute twenty-one and a half years later touched me more deeply than any other gift or expression of gratitude. To know that my contributions were appreciated by the people whose interest I had been obliged to serve with whatever talent I had was the fulfillment of all I had been taught and had strived for during my lifetime. As the bells pealed out over Honolulu, I recognized that while my active involvement in the shaping of modern Hawai'i had come to an end, the effort to provide opportunities to future generations was a living legacy I had helped to leave in these islands that I proudly call home.

Appendix A

The 442nd Veterans Club: A President Looks Back on Its First Five Years

March 25–26, 1952

NINE YEARS AGO, this organization found its roots with the formation of the 442nd Regimental Combat Team. We were then cast in an unenviable position of being of the same racial strain as the enemy who attacked Pearl Harbor. We were citizens by birth, but were we Americans who would meet the test of loyalty and patriotism by our willingness to fight and die for one's country? The draft board thought otherwise. It had by then classified us as "unwanted" citizens. But at our insistence, and the faith and promise of America that "Americanism is a matter of the heart and mind, and is not, and never was a matter of race or ancestry," the opportunity to demonstrate the soundness of this precept was given to us. We have, with the 100th Battalion that preceded us, and the Linguists and Interpreters of the Pacific, nobly met this test. Our Americanism, notwithstanding Senator Tom Connally, is borne out by the records.

Even today, six years after the termination of World War II, our achievement under fire as a unit has stood in good stead for the people of Hawai'i. The senior senator from Texas, who made the deprecating remarks on the Americanism of

Hawai'i's people, had reason to regret his intemperate and absurd statement. The people of Texas, particularly members of the 36th Division, rallied to our support. We have as members of the 442nd contributed in part to support the forceful and convincing reminder to the nation that the people of Hawai'i are proud of their citizenship and are Americans in the fullest sense of that word.

❊

The military laurels of the sons of all races of Hawai'i, of which we are a part, have dramatically been called to the attention of the American public. They compared with the best the states had to offer. But we are the heroes of the past. For today's heroes are our younger brothers again defending with valor the cause of a free world. We are the "home fronts" of yesteryear's today. Our heritage, however, compels us to respond to their call of creating conditions to ease their adjustment from soldier to civilian. We can recall our hopes and dreams of a returning soldier to a home, a family, and a job with unlimited privilege to exercise his rights to act and make known his choices as a citizen. Our fighting days are over, at least for a time, but the obligation rests on us to apply ourselves to a greater effort to realize the promise of Hawai'i.

❊

Five years have passed since the incorporation of this club. We find ourselves now, able and prepared, and in a position to tackle this job effectively and intelligently. The youthful soldier who served the cause with such vigor and stamina is no more. The years have flown, and in his place now stands a serious and mature adult schooled in the operations of the social processes of the community. The uninterrupted education for most is completed; the family is started; and the misty hopes of the past are now concrete and real. For this must be today's member of the club—with a collective record of achievement forging the bonds of a strong and cohesive unit, but willing to stand today on its participation and service to its members and community.

❄

The club by its very heritage is dedicated "to honor and esteem the supreme sacrifice made by the deceased comrades." The War Orphans Scholarship Fund, a major project to aid the children of all war dead in Hawai'i, symbolizes an adherence to this aim. The religious services, Christian and Buddhist, are our continuing obligations for memorializing them. But are these sufficient to meet this pledge? I can recall the message of Chaplain Yost at a memorial service after our last push when he challenged: "What are you as the living going to do for these fallen comrades?"

He had reached the core of our obligation to them when he pictured our cause of unsullied citizenship without reservation or question by others more fortunate by the accident of birth. We have gained that right, but will we now use that right to realize the hopes and dreams of those we left behind? This obligation today is as great as it was that day—to enter and participate, individually and collectively, in the dynamic processes of a changing society with the same high values and purposes for the general welfare of the community.

❄

We have reached a stage of development when we can participate effectively in the vital issues of today. Our increasing awareness and understanding of the forces within our community struggling for recognition and dominance compel us to do our part to indicate our stand on matters that concern us.

We cannot remain indifferent and apathetic if the club is to remain virile and purposeful. To be a mere social club with our heritage of unselfish devotion to an ideal would make mockery of the dreams of those we left behind. This is not to say that social events should not be part of our activities. They should, but they are not the end in itself.

Tangible benefits must be offered to our members, but we cannot live in a shell all our own, indifferently watching the lifestream of the community flowing by. We have too much of a stake in the future and promise of Hawai'i. We must act, and act positively, to try to resolve the problems of today. We will make mistakes. There will be frustrating failures. We may be subjected to criticism. But they do not justify inaction. If fear of mistakes and criticisms is to dictate our course of action, then the promise we had while serving a cause will be but a hollow dream. For we are a club with a purpose: to improve ourselves, our families, and our community and to live up to the promise of America. And I say this without reservation that so long as we act honestly and in good faith in accordance with the best judgment of the majority, we need not fear nor apologize to anyone.

We served as soldiers with valor, and we must not now falter in our convictions. The torch that we once carried with such distinction in battle must now shine as brightly in the battlefield of competing ideas and forces. For we are the living with a trust. We carry a name with a proud and purposeful heritage; let us keep faith with that heritage.

Appendix B

An Address to the Hawaiian Civic Clubs

February 10, 1972, Ilikai Hotel

WHEN I WAS first approached to address you, I had mixed feelings, but I consulted a friend whose judgment I valued, and he encouraged me to accept it.

So I am here this morning.

For many years I have avoided making a speech, and I was content because it was the way I wanted it.

For many years I was out of the "glassbowl of public glare"—permanently retired from the public sector—to live within a fence of privacy for myself and my family, and it was a lifestyle more to our liking. I enjoyed what I was doing in my particular fields of interests, being adequately compensated for my work with people I knew who entrusted me with such work.

But eight months ago I was thrust into the center of a stage of raging controversy within our community, and but for one public statement, I refrained from making any other statement until today.

It has been six and a half months since I took office as a trustee of the Bishop Estate. And I should like to share some of my thoughts with you.

At the outset, let me make an obvious personal commitment. You can be assured of my best efforts to perform the job I have been entrusted to do—to use whatever talents I may have to work with the other trustees of the Estate to meet the broad objectives established under the will of Princess Bernice Pauahi Paki Bishop. You can be assured that there will be no miracles—no earthshaking changes—only my continuous effort with the other trustees to enhance the assets of the Estate, and to generate more income to fund the educational activities of its principal beneficiary, Kamehameha Schools, and to assist in establishing meaningful programs in reaching out to as many of the children who are not presently receiving the benefits of her concern.

If you will allow me another brief personal note, I want to tell you of my profound admiration for the two principal bene-factors of the Estate, the princess and her husband, Charles Reed Bishop, for their foresight by creating this legacy of char-ity and compassion that shall continue in perpetuity. Trustees will come and go, but the Estate and Kamehameha Schools shall remain beyond any trustee's lifetime as the lasting mem-orial of her concern for her people.

Now, let me get back to look at this "Takabuki problem" as it may relate to you, to me, and to our broader community. You have asked, and others have asked, and rightly so, who is this guy, "Takabuki," who is vested with this awesome re-sponsibility by the Supreme Court of Hawai'i as one of her five trustees to do the good that the princess wanted for her people? What is he? An unscrupulous political hack, a shrewd conspirator out to destroy the Estate; or the best thing that has happened to the Estate; or anywhere in between these two extremes? Only time will tell how this story will end.

Perhaps, however, an observation made by a friend in half jest may be illuminating. In our abstract philosophical evalu-ation of this controversy, he sort of brightened up, grinning somewhat impishly, and said pleasantly, "You know, Matsy, I think you got a lot of charisma," and he paused, and I quickly reacted, somewhat puzzled, at this very inappropriate descrip-tion of me, especially in the midst of the raging controversy. He smiled, and continued, "Yes, a lot of *negative* charisma." How right he was! I could never win a popularity contest.

Now that you know of this speaker with negative charisma, it should warn you that you could not be expecting too much from him.

Let me, however, attempt to place in some perspective the deeper issues of this controversy by quoting from an article appearing in the *Star Bulletin* by Tomi Knaefler, in an interview with Dr. Alan Howard, a former Bishop Museum anthropologist who is now professor of anthropology at the University of Hawai'i, with a three-year live-in research and study in Nanakuli. The excerpts of his interview read as follows:

"The Takabuki protest symbolizes the Hawaiians' first battle cry to legitimize their ethnic identity. If they fail to gain it through this route, they have no choice but to express themselves through conflict—politically and militantly.

"At heart, the Hawaiian movement is no different than the blacks' fight for ethnic identity.

"The protest points up the myth of Hawai'i's melting pot concept, which, in fact, is a boiling pot of suppressed racial differences long denied legitimate airing.

"The melting pot illusion simply must go. The damage it has done is to blur ethnic diversity and to allow the Anglo culture to dominate."

These are very interesting observations. Certainly they touch the sensitive vein of ethnic identity—so different from the accepted rhetoric of the "melting pot" of the Pacific—and so true in some respects—but is this battle cry for ethnic identity comparable in intensity to the "black power" movement of the militant blacks? Is this melting pot illusion called Hawai'i similar to the black ghettos of Watts, Newark, or Harlem? Are the Japanese, or Takabuki, the symbol of suppression as the "whiteys" are to the militant blacks? Dr. Howard, however, softens this thrust by saying that:

"[But] I don't feel the protest is an expression of hostility toward the Japanese or toward Takabuki as an individual."

But is he right when he said in seeking your ethnic identity, you have "no choice but to express yourselves through conflict—politically and militantly"? Can't there be other options and alternatives that you can choose? Or can you do it alone as one ethnic group isolated from all other groups in this society? Or is this irrelevant because we are on the threshold of a new era—a changing lifestyle from the melting pot concept to ethnicity, and an emotional need of ethnic minorities to pursue militant courses of action on ethnic lines to get a "piece of the action"?

Let me try to examine this point of view.

Anyone who has lived in Hawai'i for a while can readily give you illustrations of ethnic tensions, and yes, discrimination existing in our imperfect society, but is it boiling so much that the melting pot becomes the boiling pot of suppressed racial differences? Are you, or am I, or are we prepared to move away from the goal of making Hawai'i the "melting pot" of the Pacific? Are we ready to cast aside the acceptable norm in reaching for a "homogenized blend of races," or in looking even further in the future, will there be a time when the bloodlines of our people may become so mixed as to have the "golden man" of the Pacific?

Is the "part-Hawaiian" who has grown so substantially to be this "golden man" of the future? A Hawaiian Chinese, Hawaiian Caucasian, Hawaiian Japanese, or any mixture with Hawaiian is racially classified as "part-Hawaiian," and not part-Chinese, part-*haole,* or part-Japanese. But will time and circumstances change this ethnic reference as it did in our recent Hawaiian history? I think back to the days of the 442nd Regimental Combat Team in the Second World War, and I can remember when many Hawaiian Japanese were not part-Hawaiian then, but part-Japanese who could only belong to this racially segregated combat unit. Any smattering of Japanese blood made him different from other ethnic Americans at war, but I can remember also the counterdeclaration by Franklin D. Roosevelt that "Americanism is not a matter of race, color, or creed," and for this reason this ethnic group should be given the chance to prove themselves.

What happened since is past history, and I guess we proved that President Roosevelt was not wrong that Americanism overcame ethnic bloodlines, and perhaps, the melting pot concept is viable and the "golden man" is achievable.

Are we now, two and a half decades later, involved in a new cycle of reordering our priorities when ethnic identity becomes the rallying cry for a sense of pride and confidence? Is it not true that to deny pride in one's ethnic identity is really to deny who you really are? Or, perhaps, could it be an angry ethnic outcry born of frustration? Should we now say that "brown, yellow, white, or black is beautiful," as the case may be, and put the homogenized blend of races on the back burner as a myth—the bad guy of Anglo-Saxon culture who suppresses ethnic pride?

In searching for this ethnic identity, or in seeking a sense of pride and confidence in ethnic terms, is there any danger that it may lead some to reject all that is not of its color? Or, will the opportunity to openly and proudly air their cultural and ethnic differences create an understanding, appreciation, and mutual respect among all the diverse ethnic groups to accept them as they are?

Is Dr. Howard right when he seeks replacement of the melting pot concept with ethnic diversity by saying the following?

"There are those who oppose legitimizing ethnicity on grounds this would lead to racist conflicts.

"Such danger exists more by denying ethnicity because to deny pride in one's ethnicity is to deny who you really are.

"The need then, is a society that encourages divergence, not convergence. A recognition and respect for individual differences. And a willingness to admit that there's more than one way, more than one right, more than one truth."

But what happens when such ethnicity, such way, such right, or such truth sharply conflicts with other groups aspiring for the same thing within the same society—or it runs counter to the dominant white Anglo-Saxon Protestant cultural pattern—or it denies the concept of love and the brotherhood of men of the Protestant ethic—or it violates the precept of a democratically constituted political structure that "all men are created equal"?

I guess this was our dilemma in this incident. But can there be an accommodation of both concepts?

When does ethnic identity become a divisive force, and not a positive one within a community? Can you be primarily ethnic in some areas like the Hawaiian Homes Commission, and yes, your major legacy as the Bishop Estate, Liliuokalani Trust, and others, and yet, perhaps, reconcile these as exceptions to the rule to escape the possible backlash of the accepted mores of the "melting pot" concept within our society?

Where is the balance one can strike on ethnic diversity, and yet maintain an equal, if not stronger, desire to seek a common denominator so we can live together in relative harmony? Can we believe ethnicity and the "golden man" concept at the same time? Are we, again, going through a useless exercise of soothing rhetoric of trying to blend the races even though we recognize that we will continue to have this kind of ethnic crisis so long as people have different shades of color?

Can there be a common definition of a "child of Hawai'i," a *keiki o ka aina*? Or is this, again, the same kind of rhetoric to lead to conformity to suppress ethnicity under a WASP cultural pattern?

Can anyone of us be a "child of Hawai'i" in one respect, but never in another one? Don't you, or I, or any other person, have the right to foreclose all others in doing our own ethnic thing? Isn't it your right to control your own ethnic destiny? Is it not true that only you could fully understand your own ethnic hopes and aspirations? But, then, what about a Charles Reed Bishop? Or is Abraham Lincoln irrelevant to the blacks because he was not one of them? I wonder if there are some lessons we can learn from these questions.

Or, in evaluating another incident within a different content where the converse can be said to have occurred, should we really applaud Jesse Kuhaulua for his award by the East-West Center for his contribution to intercultural activity in gaining unprecedented stature as a non-Japanese in a purely indigenous Japanese sport called sumo? Can't he be, in one way of thinking, the shining example of "brown power" over "yellow power" in Hawai'i? Or is he another example of the blending of the races, the racial tolerance, or the aloha spirit of Hawai'i? Or is Jesse Takamiyama an "Uncle Tom" for the Japanese?

I raise these hard questions to show that there are many sides to an issue, and many shades of interpretation depending on how you see it, or want to see it, and the rationale you use to justify your belief.

I raise these questions to show that any action may bring diverse reactions—good or bad, sharp or indifferent, in varying shades of intensity depending on how such action may affect the person or persons involved.

I raise these questions as a possible basis for your own critical reevaluation, and perhaps, the need for careful rethinking, reexamination, and reordering of your priorities and values— and I suggest it may be a time for soul-searching for all of us, seeking, perhaps, for a new accommodation, or reaffirming the old concepts, or blending the new and the old, in trying to reconcile all the variables covering the whole spectrum of our society, including our ethnicity, our socioeconomic priorities, our political crosscurrents, and our individual and collective hopes for the future, and seeking somehow by our actions to create a better Hawai'i for all of us.

I do not pretend to know the answers. And it is certainly not for me to try to tell you what should be done. You will have to decide what is your own way, what is your own right, and what is your own truth.

And in this difficult task that only you can decide. I wish you well.

Appendix C

*Legacy of the Princess:
An Address to the Oahu
District Council of
Hawaiian Civic Clubs*

September 11, 1976, Kamehameha Schools

THE "LEGACY OF THE PRINCESS" is a story of a concerned princess and her husband, who saw education as a means for her people to achieve their place in the sun. It is a story of an educational institution inextricably bound to land as the primary resource to support it. It is the Kamehameha Schools/ Bishop Estate, an educational trust formed to last in perpetuity.

There is no need to elaborate further on this legacy—you know all about it. We are all concerned that it continue to improve and broaden the beneficial impact on the children of this legacy through educational opportunity to achieve their highest potential in contemporary society.

While Kamehameha Schools/Bishop Estate is one entity, this direct relationship of one with the other is often ignored. Many fail to recognize, or choose to ignore, the fact that what detrimentally affects the lands of this Estate directly affects Kamehameha Schools. It is generally only organizations such as yours which are sensitive to, and concerned about, how the lands of this Estate directly affect Kamehameha Schools. It is generally only organizations such as yours which are sensitive to, and concerned about, this effect upon this legacy.

Today, as requested, I will directly address a problem affecting a substantial portion of the resources of this Estate—the effect of laws recently enacted on residential lands of this Estate.

To put this matter in proper perspective, let me define these lands for single-family residential leaseholds within the total context of the lands of the Estate in approximate acreage, income, and value ending July 1, 1975:

1. Acreage is about 5,520 acres, or about 1.6 percent of the total acreage.
2. Income generated from these lands is about $4.4 million, or about 33 percent of the gross revenues.
3. Value on the basis of 70 percent of the real property tax value is about $442 million, or about 60 percent by this method of valuation of the Estate's lands.

There are nearly 14,000 residential leases booked and recorded, primarily in Waialae-Kahala, Hawai'i Kai, Halawa, Waiau, Pearlridge, Kailua, and Heeia, and relatively few in the County of Hawai'i in Alae and Kona. Under development agreements, residential areas in Hawai'i Kai, Waialae-Iki Ridge, Waiau, Waiawa, and Heeia Meadows when and if fully developed may add several thousands more long-term single-family residential leases.

These residential lands under lease are the subject matter of legislation. They are directly affected by Chapter 516, as amended, enacted initially in 1967, and amended more recently by Act 185, Session Laws of 1975, and by Act 242, Sessions Laws of 1976. It is the substantial detrimental economic impact of these last two acts that caused us to test the validity of these laws in court on constitutional grounds under the state and federal constitutions.

Before detailing our legal position, let me try to relate the broad historical perspective of how this residential leasehold problem evolved to what it is today.

Long-term single-family residential leases started slowly about 1950 as an alternative to residential fee simple development. Wailupe, Waialae-Kahala, and older sections in Kaelepulu in Kailua were started by Bishop Estate about this time. Castle Estate started in Kailua and Kaneohe, also about this time.

Tax constraints placed on the tax-exempt status must have motivated the Estate to generate passive rental income through leases in developing its lands, together with the appreciation factor of the lands over the long term to support the increasing future needs of the schools.

With gradual acceptance of residential leaseholds by the local residents as a viable alternate to fee simple development, the availability of conventional mortgage financing by local lending institutions to build homes on these fifty-five-year leases with a twenty-five year fixed rental period, and the marketability and resale value of these residential leases gave impetus to this type of development to meet the housing needs of the community. When the FHA adopted a new policy to issue its mortgage commitment on residential leases in the early 1960s, it accelerated further in this field.

There were many pluses to residential leaseholds. The lease rental fixed for not less than twenty-five years was reasonable, and one could put the money in the house rather than house and lot in a comparatively better planned residential area of good location. I know because I went through this comparative analysis over eighteen years ago when my wife and I decided to build on a Bishop Estate leasehold lot in Tract "J" of Waialae-Kahala.

There was no real problem during the 1950s and early 1960s. The FHA and major landowners were able to agree on a mutually acceptable residential lease form. This FHA form became the basic residential lease document.

But as residential leasehold development proliferated on the lands controlled by major landowners without comparable availability in fee simple residential lots, an undercurrent for greater fee simple home ownership began developing.

The harbinger of political action to come started with the Maryland land law. It was defeated, if you recall, by one vote in the senate in the 1963 session of the legislature.

In the 1967 session, the first law for leasehold acquisition was enacted. It was more symbolic than real. Public funds through bonds could not be provided due to the bond counsel's opinion on the doubtful validity of this law. Chapter 516 stayed on the books, and amendments were made in subsequent sessions, but the funding problem continued to persist on similar legal grounds. Several years ago, a test case of the attorney general suing the director of finance of the state was started to test this question of public purpose, but it was never pursued.

Meanwhile, Bishop Estate negotiated with a Halawa group on a sale of a residential tract to a lessees' corporation based on a ruling by the Internal Revenue Service that such a transaction did not affect the tax-exempt status. Bishop Museum Tract was negotiated with First Hawaiian Bank as trustee for the lessees to purchase their individual lots with a similar ruling by the Internal Revenue Service. The Lowell Kohou remnant lots were also negotiated through the First Hawaiian Bank trust arrangement with a similar ruling by the Internal Revenue Service.

These voluntary transactions may have partially caused a slight pause in legislative action for a few years. But it was only a pause. It had popular political appeal. It was a classic case of little guys against big guys.

In addition to leasehold acquisition, lessees began pressuring elected officials for rental legislation as the fixed rental period of twenty-five years was expiring. Chapter 516 was amended by Act 185 in 1975. It arbitrarily set a rate of return on rental at 4 percent of the lessor's interest, and it set a method of acquisition based on the market value of the land less the current replacement cost of off-site improvements paid by the lessee. To avoid the funding problem through bonds, the legislature passed an appropriation of $5 million to test this leasehold acquisition law on a small tract in Manoa where nearly all the lessees indicated interest to buy.

The Hawai'i Housing Authority made the appraisal on the above formula, and the average appraisal price of the lot was about $46,000 after deducting the replacement cost of the off-site utilities paid by lessees from the market value of about $65,000, more or less, and the lessees indicated to the legislators and the Hawai'i Housing Authority that they could not afford such a price.

This set the stage for Act 242 in the 1976 session. It passed new amendments stipulating two new formulas for acquisition to further reduce the lessor's interest in the land.

1. The lessor's rental income stream and reversionary interest were discounted at 3.5 percent over insured passbook savings, or 9 percent. It should be noted at this time, the year before Act 185 set a maximum of 4 percent for rental income for at least fifteen years on renegotiation. On the basis of these acts, it is possible that the income rental stream of residential leases set at 4 percent of the lessor's interest in the land by Act 185 could be used by lessees under Act 242 for acquisition of the present worth of the lessor's interest in the land by discounting such an income stream at 9 percent. Automatically, by mathematical computation, the lessor's interest, which can be Bishop Estate, Campbell, or any other lessor with long-term residential leases, will be reduced by over 55 percent of the lessor's interest.

In some cases where a forty-year fixed rental was established at a low rate to meet the low-cost residential requirements of the FHA about ten years ago, the effect is even more severe. In Halawa, a lot having a market value of about $55,000 could be worth about $4,000 under this discounting method of valuing the present worth of the lessor's interest.

2. The second alternative formula provided new untested criteria of appraisal to increase the lessee's interest and reduce the lessor's interest in the leasehold by deducting from the market value of the land the following:

(1) value of the lease;
(2) increase in lot value from the general enhancement of neighborhood attributable to the lessee;

(3) current replacement cost of off-site improvement attributable to the lessee;
(4) increase in lot value from general enhancement of neighborhood by on-site improvements attributable to the lessee;
(5) lessee credit catchall;
(6) transfer, sales, and other costs attributable to the transaction.

This formula could be construed in many ways, and the appraisers themselves cannot agree what it really means, but the intent of these deductions clearly try to increase the lessee's interest and reduce the lessor's interest in the leasehold.

As you can readily surmise by now, Kamehameha Schools/ Bishop Estate has a huge stake, possibly involving more than $100 million, in this issue of determining the value of the lessor's and lessee's interests in these lands.

This is why the trustees are in court challenging Act 185 on lease rental control. This is why we are asking for instructions to use 9 percent as the rate for fixing rental, or in the alternative, a rental rate of 4.5 percent provided lessee agrees to a 4.5 percent discount rate under Act 242 with Hawai'i Housing Authority approval. This is why we have a moratorium on lease extensions.

We will challenge the constitutionality of these acts at every turn on every conceivable ground from "public purpose," "impairment of contract," "just compensation," "due process of law," and so on. Litigation will take time and money, but we have no alternative.

And if you have been following this matter in the newspapers, it is no longer only local, but also part of the congressional campaign. But we could not falter under any kind of pressure if we are to discharge our fiduciary duty to preserve, protect, and enhance this legacy of the princess.

You can help. The political and even the legal issue, I believe, of conversion of residential leasehold to fee simple by legislative act is possibly over. But in speaking to political office seekers of both parties, we can ask for fair and equitable treatment for Kamehameha Schools/Bishop Estate. We must be justly compensated. Let me read our testimony to the legislative housing committees of both houses of the legislature:

"We can understand the concern of the legislators in trying to make land affordable to the lessees by acquiring their residential leasehold in fee. But there is another side of the coin. The landowners also must be fairly and justly compensated for their interests in the residential leases. . . .

"We ask only, in considering any legislation involving the rent and sale of these residential leases, that the rights and interests of the landowners be fairly and justly evaluated along with the rights and interests of the lessees. . . ."

Real expression of concern by organizations such as yours on these matters, especially as they may affect this legacy of Princess Bernice Pauahi Bishop in perpetuity, will be helpful. It is not only lobbying in the legislature; the election of representatives to the House who share this concern for Kamehameha Schools is equally important.

We need your help and understanding to preserve this legacy of the princess. We can and we shall challenge these acts in court, but we will need your support in having Kamehameha Schools/Bishop Estate treated fairly by lawmakers within the political process of enacting laws.

Appendix D

Bishop Estate Today—
The Rest of You Tomorrow

July 17, 1984, Rotary Club of Honolulu

AFTER ACCEPTING THIS speaking engagement, I wondered how or what I should say. To involve you, I chose to warn you that what happened and could happen to Kamehameha Schools/Bishop Estate may also happen to you tomorrow. The impact of the recent Supreme Court decision goes beyond the publicized legal battle or the socioeconomic-political concerns of the residential leasehold conversion law. The real issue, as perceived by the *Wall Street Journal,* is that "a well intentioned court has just opened this sphere to a host of unforeseeable harassments. We may all live to regret the day we heard about the Hawaiian land reform."

First, let me step back and give you a bit of history of how this came about. With some questionable factual statements and findings of "public purpose," the state enacted a law using its power of eminent domain to take leasehold residential lots owned by the landowner-lessor and transfer them to the lessees solely for their private use and benefit. On constitutional grounds, we resisted this involuntary conversion of our residential leases by the state. We lost in the federal district court. We appealed to the ninth circuit court and won. The state appealed, and the Supreme Court of the United States overruled the ninth circuit court.

211

It is now the law of the land that any governmental entity can use its power of eminent domain to take private property from *A* and transfer it to *B* solely for *B*'s private use and benefit so long as such taking can be "rationally related to a conceivable public purpose." It substituted this broad "conceivable public purpose" test for the ninth circuit court's view of this leasehold conversion law that "it was the intention of the framers of the Constitution and the Fifth Amendment that this form of majoritarian tyranny should not occur." It decreed, also, that "public use" is no longer a requirement in the use of this awesome power of condemnation under the Fifth Amendment.

Maybe now under this decision, Oakland may have a case in keeping the Oakland Raiders in Oakland, or Baltimore its Baltimore Colts.

My colleague, Dick Lyman, gave it a biblical perspective when he said that the leasehold conversion law not only encourages you to covet that which is thy neighbor's; it also helps you to take it from him.

The covetous people are now smelling blood. We can expect them to launch a massive assault on private property by convincing the legislature to use the power of eminent domain to redistribute any and all land ownership in Hawai'i. We already see signs of this here.

Condominium and townhouse lessees, Big Island agricultural lessees, lessees along Airport Row and Campbell Industrial Park are among the first of those who are organizing for an appeal to the legislature to extend the scope of this statute to include land in multifamily, agricultural, industrial, and commercial uses.

This is scary. As I stated at the outset, we are not alone. Your property may be next. The threat of "majoritarian tyranny" through the political process is in fact upon us. The judiciary has seemingly abdicated its responsibility to define what constitutes legitimate public purpose and use in the taking of private property under the Constitution and the Fifth Amendment. The only protection against this kind of punitive law by the political majority is the broad constitutional test that such taking by condemnation be "rationally related to a conceivable public purpose" by the legislative body.

Let me again repeat the position of the trustees of this Estate. No one is doing us any favor in forcing us to sell our lands, including residential leasehold lots.

Word filters back to us that many purportedly knowledgeable people are telling lawmakers and the media that "this law benefits the Estate." They say, "The trustees may not be smart enough to know it, but we are doing this for their own good." Don't do us any favors. The tax benefits accruing to private taxable trusts are not applicable to us. Reinvestment privileges of condemnation proceeds, capital gains vis-à-vis ordinary income, liquidity for substantial estate taxes are not taxable concerns of a tax-exempt entity. We don't need this law. The simplistic numbers game of current yield, present worth, and compounding interest to rationalize the taking of a Hawaiian legacy is not justified. On a total return concept of yield and appreciation, we are convinced that real estate is preferable to stocks and bonds over a comparable holding period. Land has served the Kamehameha Schools/Bishop Estate well. In fact, so well that now others would have the state use its condemnation power to take the land away.

The Hawaiian community remembers Lunalilo Estate. It sold its lands around Kapiolani, Diamond Head, and Kaimuki after the king's death in 1874, and then invested the remaining proceeds in mortgages, securities, and government bonds. Compare it today with Bishop Estate. Had Lunalilo directed its trustees, as Princess Pauahi Bishop did, to retain the land and sell it only as necessary to run the home for the aged, the Lunalilo Trust today would rival the Bishop Estate in its net asset value, and it would be able to assist many more than the approximately fifty elderly Hawaiians who now live in Lunalilo Home.

Princess Pauahi was wise when she directed her trustees to retain the "Aina," her primary endowment, and sell it only when necessary for the Kamehameha Schools or the best interest of the trust. Real estate has been, and will continue to be, a sound, prudent, long-term investment.

But we have no option on residential leaseholds at this moment. And if we must sell as required by law, then the state through the HHA should take a more impartial stance than it did on the first case tried before the first circuit court. The HHA should have its own independent appraisal by a MAI appraiser selected by it. It did not do so in the first case, and the jury returned with a price of about 18 percent of the fee simple market value of the lot. My colleague, Myron Thompson, called this a "rip-off," and we concur. It is much too low. On day one after a lessee acquires our leased fee interest at 18 percent of market value, he has a very substantial windfall over his acquisition cost of his lot.

As unfairly low as this kind of jury-determined price is, the lessees are now proposing a lease rent control act to the legislature that can on an income approach method of valuation substantially lower the value of our interest even more. This would be confiscatory.

This, again, is a classic case of punitive action against major landowners. The pattern is the same. Where the land rent under the lease is favorable to the lessee, the landowner is forced to abide by it, but when the lease rent is perceived to be unfavorable to the lessees under the leases, then a change of the law is proposed to favor the lessees. Do you wonder why we sometimes seem paranoid? We are in a no-win situation. In votes, the lessees greatly outnumber landowners, and we know the survival instincts of those in politics are understandably strong. This majoritarian threat is real. And we see little judicial relief under the recent Supreme Court decision.

To survive in this kind of political and judicial network, and to stop this kind of punitive "rip-off" of major dimensions to the Estate, we need help. We had better mobilize the Hawaiian community to balance the political scale. If they want to preserve their legacy, they may have to toll the bells of Kawaiahao Church, march around the Kamehameha statue and capitol, and picket the legislature to express their deep concerns, and perhaps, to vent their anger and frustration against those trying to break up their legacy. They reacted in somewhat similar fashion at my appointment twelve years ago, and they should do no less now to protect and preserve their most important Hawaiian legacy.

And if you think this is only a Hawaiian legacy's problem, think again. You already hear rumbling by other lessees to expand the scope of this law. The condominiums and agricultural land leases are on the hit list of some elected officials. With the legal sanction seemingly given by the Supreme Court, the conservation movement against private property is only beginning in the legislature.

With this kind of threat, Hawai'i deserves its anti-business and anti–property owner images. All of the political rhetoric otherwise does not really help. Action does speak louder than words. We see it only becoming worse. In this kind of climate, we have little choice but to look outside Hawai'i. Our discretionary investment dollars are being placed elsewhere. Prudent business judgment dictates this type of action. This hurts us. Our roots are here. We are all *keiki-oka-aina.* We love Hawai'i, but we feel unwelcome. This is but another instance where we are being treated like "strangers in our own land."

We will, however, always have a presence in Hawai'i as long as we are allowed to keep our lands. We are aware that our lands are exposed to the awesome power of condemnation by the state, which is limited only by the broad constitutional test that taking be "rationally related to a conceivable public purpose." Under this kind of continuing threat, reinvestment in Hawai'i should be imprudent. We hope this changes, but we do not see any tangible indication as yet.

We will cooperate whenever possible with the public and private sectors to try to resolve problems of mutual concern. We will try, as our roots are here. Our fiduciary duty requires us to preserve, protect, and enhance the endowment of this Estate to achieve one mission, and this mission is "to offer as many meaningful educational opportunities as resources will permit for the beneficiaries, giving preference to children and youth of whole and part-Hawaiian ancestry, to assist them in their efforts to develop their highest potential as effective participants in society."

Our goal is no more or no less. In this respect, let me say that for all those who believe that they hurt the trustees when they take punitive actions against the Estate, they are wrong. They are only hurting the Kamehameha Schools and all the Hawaiian children now and in the future, who enjoy the fruits of this legacy.

One last word, and this brings us full circle: if you have private property, and not necessarily land, coveted by others, be careful. What happened and could happen to Kamehameha Schools/Bishop Estate could also happen to you. The *Wall Street Journal* may be correct when it said, "We may all live to regret the day when we heard about the Hawai'i land reform."

Mahalo.

Appendix E

Speech to National AJA Veterans Reunion

June 30, 1990, Kona, Hawai'i

FRED FUJIMOTO ASKED and I accepted his invitation to speak to you on our role—the role of nisei veterans in today's world. When I refer to "nisei veterans," I mean "us," the men of the 100th Battalion, the 442nd Regimental Combat Team, the Military Intelligence Group, the 1399th Battalion, and other members of the armed forces of World War II, spanning a period of four and a half decades.

To try to find our special niche today and to find and place our role as veterans in perspective, we need to look back on how we became what we are. We begin with our issei parents, who came to this new and strange land as second and third sons of poor farm families to earn and save enough money and return home to Japan.

I can think of no better way of describing their hopes and dreams before they came, their struggle and disappointment in the cane fields after they came, than the haunting and mournful song created by the *Kanyaku Imin*—the first contract labor from Japan to work in the sugarcane fields in Hawai'i. It captures the essence of the dreams they had, the sweat and tears and struggle they endured as they labored in the canefields, and finally the roots they established in this new and strange land. It translates like this:

Hawai'i, Hawai'i, like a dream so I came.
But now I shed my tears in the canefields.
I cut the cane, my wife strips the leaves, *huli, huli.*

Our sweat and tears we get by.
To go on to America, or to return to Japan,
that is the problem in Hawai'i.
I cried when I sailed out of Yokohama.
But now I have children and even grandchildren.

We are the children of this song, and the grandchildren are our children, whose roots were planted here by them.

I am sure it was no different for those isseis who went on to America. Their struggle in the harsh and hostile environment was created by the yellow jingoistic press, the Alien Land Laws that denied ownership of land to them, and the many other racially related roadblocks placed before them, but they too survived by their sweat and tears and established their roots for their children and grandchildren.

As citizens by birth, remember how we were taught in school to believe in the American dream—a nation that declared its national purpose as embodied in the Declaration of Independence with the right of each person to "life, liberty, and the pursuit of happiness"; the Constitution of the United States with the Bill of Rights to assure individual rights for each person who lived here; and the Gettysburg Address of Lincoln describing our form of government as "the government of the people, for the people, and by the people"?

Remember, also, how the nisei leaders of this period were pushing us to become the clones of the white, Anglo-Saxon, Protestant American? Americanism was the goal. Assimilation, loyalty, and patriotism were the buzzwords. Even though our parents could not become naturalized Americans, we were told to believe, and we believed. We were American citizens, no better, no worse, and no different from any other American citizens.

Then the war came without warning on December 7, 1941, when Japan attacked Pearl Harbor, and our world changed from that date forward. All the rhetoric of citizenship and the rights and privileges of individuals were shattered by this one event. Suddenly our most significant and overriding characteristic was our identical ethnicity with our Japanese enemy. It made little difference whether we were citizens or aliens, male or female, adult or child. We were Japanese.

On the West Coast, while it was not the Holocaust of the Jewish concentration camp of Hitler's Germany, persons solely by reason of being Japanese ethnically were herded into hastily built camps surrounded by barbed wire and guarded by soldiers with guns. War power superseded any and all rights of persons of Japanese ancestry on the West Coast, and all the ugly emotions of xenophobia, bigotry, and prejudice aroused by fear and suspicion showed in this racially motivated act.

Those of us in Hawai'i were more fortunate. For various reasons—economics, logistics, a more tolerant society— people like Jack Burns and Kendall Fielder were able to persuade the military that sending all of us to Molokai or other encampments was counterproductive.

But we were under surveillance. Like all citizens of Japanese ancestry, we were ineligible for the draft. We were "unwanted" by our own country at war because of ethnicity.

Many of us felt betrayed, but we were pretty helpless. But somehow cool heads prevailed in time. Rationality returned. The powers to be were persuaded that an opportunity should be given to niseis to prove that "Americanism is a matter of the heart and mind, and Americanism is not and never was a matter of race and ancestry." This gave birth to the 442nd Regimental Combat Team.

The rest is history. The 100th Battalion and the 442nd Regimental Combat Team came home from Europe as war heroes with combat badges, medals, ribbons, and awards as the most decorated unit in the United States Army's history. The Military Intelligence Group, or the "Yankee Samurais," who were belatedly credited by the Pacific Command for their significant contribution to shortening the war against Japan, demonstrated individual and collective courage and heroism in the Pacific theater.

The isseis gave their sweat and tears in setting their roots in America for us, and as their children, we earned our place for ourselves and future generations with our sweat, tears, and a "helluva" lot of our blood. Each generation has paid a price to earn their place in our multiethnic American society.

In Hawai'i, the returning nisei veterans educated through the GI Bill of Rights entered and challenged the political, economic, and social establishments of Hawai'i with a vengeance.

From this boiling cauldron of activity rose nisei veterans like Dan Inouye (442nd) and Spark Matsunaga (100th) in the U.S. Senate, and George Ariyoshi (MIS) as governor of the State of Hawai'i. Others achieved success and recognition in public offices, elected and appointed, in the judiciary, in the business and professional fields. On the mainland, similar strides of substantial success were made in politics, in education, in the judiciary and business.

And when we look back to where we were and where we are today, we've come a long way in two generations. Perhaps the most symbolic victory of all was that you *kotonks* won the battle on reparations for internment. And, let me add, the "buddhaheads" from Hawai'i also savor your victory.

But the years have taken their toll. Senator Matsunaga recently passed away. We are now in our sixties and seventies. We have passed the prime of our life. Time has been catching up with us.

But there is one area of concern where our age should not be a factor. We may need to gear up and do battle again. In recent years, I sense again a disturbing phenomenon of rising signs of anti-Asian racism. Two white unemployed autoworkers attacked and killed a Chinese American with baseball bats, thinking he was Japanese, and the pair were merely sentenced to three years' probation. Or, when Vietnamese fishermen were attacked, and their nets destroyed, for working longer and harder than their local white competitors. Or the anti-Asian feeling recently shown by the blacks against Korean-operated groceries in New York as a result of a dispute with a black woman customer.

I have an uncomfortable feeling of rising xenophobic tendency when one media poll indicates that the American public considers the economic threat of Japan is greater than a military threat of communistic Russia to the well-being of the United States.

Much of what is happening is more subtle xenophobia than the clear and unequivocal racism of the internment decision. This phenomenon, perhaps, is more understandable as perceptively observed by writer Richard Condon: "It's just so much easier to create an enemy out of people who don't look like Aunt Mary."

Polls show "Japanese bashing" is popular and acceptable by the public. Politicians blame those "who don't look like Aunt Mary" as the probable causes of our problems. There are disturbing hints of political demagoguery. This is not to say some criticisms are not deserved, but I sense an uncomfortable rise of racism against those who don't look like Aunt Mary.

If there is a role we can play in the twilight of our lives, it is to fight this kind of racism and bigotry. If there is any spirit left in us, we can again carry the torch to support the weak and unprotected, and those charged with guilt by identity and association, especially when directed by the powerful against those who don't look like Aunt Mary. It may be our "last hurrah," and it could be challenging and worthwhile. Maybe we could wave the flag again.

If I sound as though I am sermonizing, please forgive me. But I believe it is our obligation as nisei veterans who experienced racism and bigotry to ensure that such mistakes of the past are not repeated again in whatever form they take. We are especially obligated to combat xenophobic actions against those who don't look like Aunt Marys by the Aunt Marys of our society.

We owe this to ourselves, our children, and the future generation, and, yes, at the risk of sounding too hopelessly idealistic, or like Don Quixote reaching for the stars in his "impossible dream," we should keep trying again to achieve our American dream of tolerance and justice for all.

Appendix F

1991 Kamehameha Schools/Bishop Estate Service Awards

August 20, 1991, Keʻelikolani Auditorium

WELCOME BACK TO the annual service award get-together as we prepare to begin Kamehameha's 105th school year.

Looking back, one realizes how quickly time flies. Twenty years have passed since I came on board. That was the year 1971.

As we know, KS/BE was originally created under the will of Princess Bernice Pauahi Bishop over a century ago, and as we were constituted then, in 1971 when I first started, as we are now, and as we will be in the future, we are first and foremost an educational institution. Our mission is education, that is to say, we are committed to provide as many meaningful educational opportunities to qualified beneficiaries as our resources will permit.

While this ultimate educational mission is clear and unequivocal, the implementation of this mission rests primarily with you—the president and the supporting administrative staff, the principals, counselors, and teachers on the front lines, to educate the continual flow of student beneficiaries. We could not forget you who house, feed, transport, secure, build, repair, and clean the school facilities as important contributors toward achieving this mission.

Today, however, let me speak briefly about the other side of our institution—the resources that serve as the engine to keep

222

the Kamehameha system operating as a viable educational institution.

It is important, first, to recognize that our resources are limited. There is no limitless fund. We must plan and match operating revenues with costs to preserve our asset base. Programs must be meaningful and cost-effective to justify our expenditures. If we are to continually improve and expand these programs, we must plan prudently and realistically with our asset base intact to generate revenues to meet this need in perpetuity.

Let me give you a short comparative history of the past twenty years. In 1971, the gross income was slightly more than $8 million. The net income before costs of operating the schools was slightly more than $5 million, and the costs of operating the schools after deducting tuition and fees was about $6.3 million. In 1971, without development costs, recoveries, and sale of land, we were operating in deficit as we were several years before. We were a classic example of being land-rich but cash-poor during these years.

Luckily, we were able to turn the corner slowly at first and more rapidly later so that today we are in good, solid financial shape. At the end of the last fiscal year, the net costs of operating the schools increased about seven times, to more than $44 million, while the net operating revenues increased about twentyfold over the past twenty years. Our asset base, particularly our liquidity, also appreciated substantially over the past two decades, and if we continue on the same course as we did in the past decade, the funding for the educational mission from income will be sustainable and achievable in the future.

Let me give you a little flavor of the asset management of our portfolio—what we are doing now and what we see happening to our asset base in the future.

By now you have heard that KS/BE has begun a program of selling some of our residential leasehold condominium lands. Actually, what we are doing is redeploying a portion of our assets into higher-yielding investments with real appreciation potential. Such redeployment will be less vulnerable to sociopolitical pressure from the larger community. By capturing the value of the asset now—at prices set on what we determine to be the fair value of our interest, and not the value set by governmental formulas favoring and skewed toward the lessees—we will realize a greater economic benefit than we would if we were forced to liquidate our interest under another mandatory leasehold conversion law.

Another news item you may have read recently was our purchase of the Windward Mall. Consistent with our policy to expand our position in income-producing commercial properties, we saw Windward Mall as an extremely attractive investment in terms of current yield and future appreciation. And this is comparable to our other commercial investment properties, such as Royal Hawaiian Shopping Center, Keauhou Shopping Village, Waiakamilo Business Center, and Kawaiahao Plaza.

We have also positioned ourselves for what will occur in the more distant future. Pearlridge Shopping Center and Kahala Mall will be owned outright by this institution one day in the future as will a number of smaller shopping centers, such as Koko Marina and other shopping and commercial centers in Hawai'i Kai and Kamehameha Shopping Center just down the hill. We have Royal Hawaiian Shopping Center, Inc., a wholly owned subsidiary, which will manage our shopping centers, office buildings, and industrial properties when the time comes to take over these properties located on our lands.

The media has also mentioned that the sale of HonFed Bank was being negotiated. If consummated, our return on this investment will be substantial. It could surpass the gains we realized from First Hawaiian Bank's buyout of our interest in First Interstate Bank. Without any fanfare, we recently sold our minority interest in an offshore reinsurance company to a major Swiss insurance company for even greater gains than the other two investments above.

While most of our investments are performing as well as can be expected in this recessionary and slow-growth environment, we do have several troubled investments. Turnarounds, however, are expected with workouts and restructuring of excessive debt by equity infusion and conversion of debt to equity, better management, and the likely economic rebound from the recession. And at worst, this exposure is easily manageable within the context of our overall portfolio.

In the past decade, we formed close relationships with some of the largest educational and charitable foundations in the country. We have investment partners like Duke University, University of Texas, Harvard University, and Yale. And we have a close affiliation with the MacArthur Foundation, perhaps one of the largest and most prestigious private foundations in America. We have working relationships with nationally known investment bankers such as Goldman Sachs and J. P. Morgan Bank. National credit rating bureaus such as Standard & Poor's and Moody's monitor our financial status. Wall Street is aware of our investment activities. (Ironically, Wall Street may know us better than Merchant Street here.)

We have an established national credit rating so we could issue short-term commercial paper. It is the highest rating— P-1 by Moody's and A1+ by Standard & Poor's—allowing us to issue commercial paper now at about 250 basis points below prime. In fact, our strong credit allows us to earn millions in other ways. We arbitrage our cost of borrowing with the preferred rate of return set in our real estate investments. We enhance credit to bank loans to investment entities in which we are involved by arbitraging interest rate differentials. In addition, we negotiate commitment fees and equity kickers for these credit enhancements. We are utilizing the strength and power of our financial muscle.

But the core of our economic strength and growth still is and will continue to be the real estate in Hawai'i.

Our crown jewel is the sixteen acres in Waikiki on which sits the Royal Hawaiian and Sheraton Waikiki Hotels, and our own Royal Hawaiian Shopping Center. Two years ago in arbitration, the land next door was valued at $1,200 per square foot—over $52 million per acre. On this basis, our Waikiki land is valued at more than $750 million.

You've read about the renegotiation of rent for Kahala Hilton, and the lessee crying to the media about the substantial increase of lease rental he faces at current market value. But don't feel sorry for him. He had a tremendous bargain and windfall for several decades of extremely low lease rental, and he never offered to share this windfall with us. His day of reckoning has finally arrived, but even then once the rent is set, it is set for ten years at the same rent. And if inflation is considered, he pays less due to erosion of the dollar value for each succeeding year of this period. He still has a good deal.

In the past decade, we've seen prime urban land values in places like Kakaako rise to more than $300 per square foot, and Kapalama to over $100 per square foot. And our positions in other urban commercial properties located within the city had similar appreciation of value. In time, with the low cost of financing from commercial paper and medium-term notes, and the availability of prime urban lands as in Kakaako, and later in Kapalama, a planned mixed-use redevelopment of office, commercial, and retail buildings can be structured by KS/BE and managed by our wholly owned subsidiary. This should give us an asset base of income-producing commercial properties far beyond what we have now.

This can be done slowly and prudently. Rental income will continue while we wait. We have time on our side. We have the lands and sources of funds available. We can and should be able to survive the media bashing, the critical self-proclaimed "experts," political bias and showboating, and the economic ups and downs. We can redevelop these properties on a timetable we deem best for KS/BE.

We need, also, to look for other investment opportunities besides real estate in Hawai'i. Positions taken in First Interstate Bank and HonFed are illustrations of such investment opportunities available here. At the same time, we need to diversify in kind and place to balance our investment portfolio. We must look for investment opportunities outside Hawai'i. We can as we are already known in the national investment community. Our credit rating is excellent. Our credibility is good. With our working relationships with major educational and charitable institutions, investment bankers, and business groups, the way is already paved for continual deal flows. With these institutional affiliations, also, we have knowledgeable support to compare, evaluate, and confirm jointly the risks–

rewards of these investment opportunities. Today, we are one of the significant players in this specialized field of investments by major tax-exempt institutions. In fact, in real estate, I believe we are on the leading edge among these institutions.

For example, through our subsidiary, we own a half interest in over three hundred thousand acres in Upper Michigan. To land bank for the long term, we are presently negotiating to buy more timberland and lake frontage on Lake Superior, which will more than double our acreage there. If we do so, we will have in Upper Michigan more than double our total land acreage in Hawai'i. But, as we know, size alone is not the critical factor. Our crown jewel of sixteen acres in Waikiki is valued at more than eight times this total contemplated acquisition. But in the long term, this acquisition may have an even greater upside potential percentage wise than Waikiki. Also, we are diversifying and balancing our land ownership in kind and place, and such land is not subject to, or dependent on, the sociopolitical and economic conditions of Hawai'i. This should remind us again that everything is relative, and investments, especially land, must be judged accordingly with all the variables in mind.

Another area we are now looking at is the investment opportunities in the Pacific Basin. We have a small investment in Xiamen Bank in the Fujian Province of the People's Republic of China with the Chinese governmental agencies, Asian Development Bank, Long Term Credit Bank of Japan, and the Simon Group. This interesting affiliation can be the nexus to open other investment and merchant banking opportunities in the Asian market.

On a long-term macro basis, there is no question that the Pacific Basin is the area of growth. The next century, it has been said, will be the Pacific era. We are well situated. We have meaningful contacts in Japan, Hong Kong, and the People's Republic of China. We can be the Hawaiian catalyst for meaningful economic relationships with various Asian and Asean entities within the Pacific Basin.

As I draw on my twenty years here, I am encouraged by the future prospect of this institution. The future is bright. We are giving our students a first-rate education. We are reaching out to fill the niche of preschool education. We are expanding our counseling of at-risk children. We are providing scholarship funds for post–high school education, not only to graduates at the schools but to graduates of public school. We are expanding the educational opportunities to as many qualified beneficiaries as our resources will permit. We are keeping faith with the legacy of the princess.

The asset base is sound and growing in value each year. It will continue to generate the funds needed for the planned future growth of the schools. We must, however, continually match costs with revenues without eroding the asset base if we are to continue to improve on our moving mission target in perpetuity.

Everyone in this institution has a part to play. The princess started this institution with her legacy. It is our obligation and challenge to preserve this legacy in perpetuity, constantly improving and expanding the educational opportunities to as many qualified beneficiaries as our resources will permit.

With your understanding and help, I know we can do it.

Imua Kamehameha.

Chronology

Feb. 25, 1923	Born in Haleiwa, a part of the sugar plantation community of Waialua on Oahu, Territory of Hawai'i, US.
June 1937	First paid employment to weed in the cane fields of the sugar plantation.
June 1940	Graduated from Waialua High School, in Waialua, Oahu.
Sept. 1940	Moved to Honolulu from Haleiwa to attend the University of Hawai'i's Teachers College.
June 1941	Worked full-time at Fort Armstrong, Honolulu, and attended University of Hawai'i at night as part-time student.
Jan. 1942	Reenrolled as full-time student at the University of Hawai'i.
March 1943	Volunteered for the 442nd Regimental Combat Team and left for infantry training in Camp Shelby, Mississippi.
July 1943	Met Ayako Saiki in Chicago, Illinois, while on a three-day pass from Camp Shelby.
Oct. 1944	Sailed to the European theater to join the 442nd Regimental Combat Team.
June 1945	After VE day in Europe, returned to the United States to enter the Military Interpreters School in Fort Snelling, Minnesota.

Nov. 1945	With enough points for discharge from prior combat service, discharged from the army at Fort Kamehameha on Oahu, Territory of Hawai'i.
Jan. 1946	Returned to Chicago to apply for admission to the University of Chicago Law School.
	Married Ayako Saiki.
March 1946	Began four-year program at the University of Chicago Law School.
March 1949	Graduated from the University of Chicago with a J.D. degree.
May 1949	Returned to Hawai'i on the *Lurline,* which was the last ship to dock in Honolulu before the ILWU's six-month dock strike.
Aug. 1949	Started working at the Unemployment Compensation Bureau, Department of Labor, Territory of Hawai'i.
Oct. 1949	Passed the bar examination of Hawai'i, and received licenses to practice law in the State of Hawai'i and the federal courts of the United States.
Jan. 21, 1951	Birth of son Glen S. Takabuki.
Jan. 1952	Started private law practice with Ben Takayesu.
March 1952	Elected president of the 442 Veterans Club.
May 1952	Member of the "Connally Caravan," representing the nisei war veterans of World War II, went to protest the derogatory racial remarks about Hawai'i's people by the senator of Texas.
Nov. 1952	Elected to the Board of Supervisors, City and County of Honolulu, State of Hawai'i.
Feb. 25, 1953	Birth of daughter, Beth K. Takabuki.
March 1953	Represented Chinn Ho on the Lewers Street apartment project.
Nov. 1954	Reelected to the Board of Supervisors, City and County of Honolulu.

May 17, 1956	Birth of daughter, Anne M. Takabuki.
Nov. 1956	Reelected to the Board of Supervisors, City and County of Honolulu.
Nov. 1958	Reelected to the Board of Supervisors, City and County of Honolulu.
Aug. 1959	Hawai'i admitted as the fiftieth state of the United States.
Oct. 1959	First trip to Japan, representing a client in Honolulu who wanted to lease land to a major department store in Tokyo.
Nov. 1960	Reelected to the Board of Supervisors, City and County of Honolulu.
Oct. 1962	Worked on John A. Burns' campaign for governor of the State of Hawai'i.
Nov. 1962	Reelected to the City Council, City and County of Honolulu.
Nov. 1962	Army goodwill tour to Taiwan, Hong Kong, Naha, Okinawa, Hiroshima City, Hiroshima, Seoul, South Korea and Tokyo, Japan, with mayor of the City and County of Honolulu, representing the City Council.
Dec. 1962	Represented Chinn Ho in the development of Ilikai, the first major condominium project in Hawai'i, and secured long-term financing by a major U.S. institutional lender.
Nov. 1964	Reelected to the City Council, City and County of Honolulu.
Nov. 1968	Lost reelection to the City Council, City and County of Honolulu.
June 1972	Appointed by the Supreme Court of Hawai'i to be trustee of Kamehameha Schools/Bishop Estate.
Aug. 1972	Began continuous tenure as trustee until date of retirement.

Oct. 1991	Spoke at the Great Hall of China (Beijing) as one of the foreign partners of the Xiamen International Bank joint venture.
April 1992	Negotiated purchase of equity interest in Goldman Sachs.
Feb. 1993	Mandatory retirement at age seventy as trustee of Kamehameha Schools/Bishop Estate.

Index